THE
FIX-IT
BOOK

ISBN: 0-88176-306-3

Cover Design: Jeff Hapner

CONTENTS

INTRODUCTION

How many times have you put off a home repair job just because you weren't exactly sure how to do it? Truth is, most fix-it projects are a lot easier than you might think. To replace the washer on a dripping faucet, for example, you need only a screwdriver and wrench, and 15 minutes or less of your time.

Not every home repair is quite that easy, of course, but almost all of the 39 fix-it jobs in this book can be pulled off in an hour or so—at a tiny fraction of what you'd pay a professional to do the work. You don't need any complicated or expensive tools, either; in fact, you probably already have most of the tools you'll need.

From painting to plumbing, basement to roof, THE FIX-IT BOOK prescribes remedies for ills that afflict just about every house or apartment. Try your hand at a repair or two and you'll soon find yourself turning to these pages for other ways to get your home ship-shape and keep it that way.

CURING SQUEAKY FLOORS AND STAIRS

Squeaky floors aren't serious structural problems, but they can be very annoying. If your floors are exposed hardwood, you might be able to stop a squeak by sprinkling talcum powder over the noisy boards and sweeping it back and forth to force it down into the cracks. The powder will lubricate the edges of the boards, eliminating the noise. For a more permanent repair, tackle the squeak with the procedure explained here.

If there's a basement or crawl space under the noisy floor, work from this area to locate the problem. You'll need a helper upstairs to walk on the squeaky spot while you work. Watch the subfloor under the noisy boards. If the subfloor

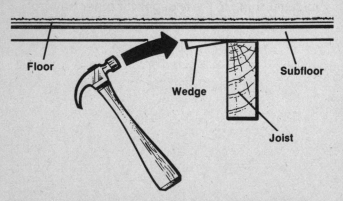

Working under the floor, look for gaps between the joists and the subfloor. Drive wedges into the gaps to keep the floor from moving, and to stop the squeaks.

moves visibly, or if you can pinpoint the noise, outline the affected areas with chalk. At the joists closest to your outlines, look for gaps between the joist and the subfloor; wherever there's a gap, the floorboards can move. To stop squeaks here, pound thin wedges into the gaps to stop the movement; shingles or wood shims make good wedges.

If there are no gaps along the joists, or if the squeaks are coming from an area between the joists, there's probably a gap between the floorboards and the subfloor. To pull the two layers together, drive wood screws up into the squeaky areas; drill pilot holes before inserting the screws. The wood screws must be long enough to penetrate into the floor above you, but make sure they aren't so long that they go all the way through the boards—if this happens, you'll end up with sharp screw points sticking up from your floor.

If you can't get at the floor from underneath, you'll have to work from the top, with spiral flooring nails. Locate the squeak and try to determine whether it's at a joist or between joists. To eliminate

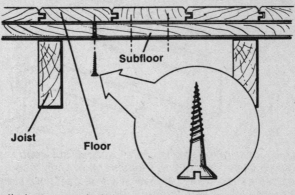

To eliminate squeaks between joists, drill pilot holes and drive wood screws up through the subfloor and the floorboards to pull the layers together.

the squeak, drive two spiral flooring nails, angled toward each other in a V, through the floorboards and the subfloor; at a joist, use longer spiral flooring nails, and drive them through the floorboards and the subfloor and into the joist. Drill pilot holes before driving the nails; countersink the nail heads with a nail set, and cover them with wood filler.

If the floor is tiled or carpeted, and you can't get at the floorboards from above or below, you probably won't be able to eliminate the squeak without removing the floor covering. Before you do this, try to reset the loose boards by pounding. Using a hammer and a block of scrap wood as a buffer, pound the floor firmly over the squeaky boards, in an area about two or three feet square. The pressure of the pounding may force loose nails back into place.

Squeaky stairs can be eliminated with graphite powder sprinkled from the top, or with wedges or wood blocks secured with glue and finishing nails to the stairs' underside.

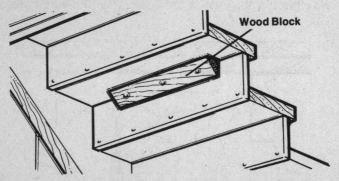

Wood Block

If stair joints are too small to admit wedges, cut wood blocks to fit into the joints under the stairs. Apply wood glue to the sides of the blocks that will contact the stairs; secure the blocks with finishing nails.

REPLACING VINYL FLOOR TILES

Damaged vinyl tiles are easy to reglue or replace. Tiles that are loose or curled up at the corners can be reglued. First, however, cover the loose tile with aluminum foil and spread a clean rag or small towel on the foil. Using moderate heat, press the edges of the loose tile with an iron to soften the old adhesive. Carefully lift *only* the edges of the tile with a putty knife and scrape off the old mastic.

To reglue the tile, spread a thin layer of mastic on the cleaned area, scraping any excess adhesive off. Press the tile back into place, smoothing it from center to edges. Cover the entire tile with a piece of scrap wood and weight it with a gallon can of paint or other heavy object. Leave the weight in place for the entire curing period of the new mastic, as recommended by the manufacturer.

To remove a tile, warm it with a propane torch fitted with a flame-spreader nozzle; be careful not to damage surrounding tiles. Pry up the edges and lift the tile off. Allow mastic under the tile to harden before scraping it off.

Damaged or badly stained tiles are removed entirely. Warm the damaged tile carefully with a propane torch, or press with an iron over a clean rag and aluminum foil. Being careful not to damage surrounding tiles, pry up the edges of the damaged tile and lift it off. Allow the mastic left under the tile to harden and then scrape it off.

If heat doesn't loosen the damaged tile, you can use cold. Wearing work gloves, cover the damaged tile with dry ice and allow it to stand for 5 to 10 minutes, then remove any remaining dry ice. The damaged tile should be cold and very brittle. Starting in the middle of the tile, use a hammer and chisel to split the tile and pry out the pieces. Work from the center to the edges, being careful not to chip surrounding tiles. Scrape the floor under the tile to remove all old mastic.

Before gluing down the replacement tile, make sure it fits the opening precisely. If it binds at the edges or overlaps the surrounding tiles, smooth the edges carefully with sandpaper. Mark matching edges with a gease pencil to make sure you replace the tile correctly.

With a notched trowel, spread a thin layer of mastic in the opening for the new tile. Set one edge of the tile in place and lower it into the prepared opening. The new tile should be level with the rest of the floor. If it's too high, press firmly to squeeze out excess mastic; if it's too low, lift the tile and apply more mastic and weight the new tile for the full curing time of the mastic.

REPAIRING VINYL SHEET FLOORING

Scratches, holes, and worn spots in resilient sheet flooring are easy to repair.

Scratches and dents. Make a patching compound to fill deep scratches and dents in resilient flooring. You can do this by bending a small piece of scrap flooring sharply, top surface out. Holding the bent piece of flooring over a shallow pan, scrape the bend with a sharp utility knife to produce a fine powder. Scrape only as deep as the surface color; rebend the scrap flooring as you work to keep the scrapings a uniform color. Scrape enough powder to more than fill the hole or scratch.

Add a few drops of clear nail polish to the scrapings and mix to a thick paste. Use masking tape to cover and protect the area around the scratch or hole to be filled.

Apply the vinyl paste to the scratch with a putty knife, smoothing the surface carefully. Let it dry for about an hour, and then remove the tape around the patch. Using grade 000 steel wool, buff the patch to make it shiny.

Large holes. Patch large holes and worn spots with scrap pieces of flooring. Choose a piece larger than the hole and set it over the bad spot. Align the pattern of the patch exactly with the pattern on the floor; then, being careful not to move the patch, tape it firmly to the floor, all around the edges, with package sealing tape—not masking tape.

Using a sharp utility knife and a steel straightedge, cut a rectangular patch from the taped-down piece of flooring. The patch must be larger than the hole underneath it. If the floor has a pattern of bricks or other regular shapes, cut along joints or lines as much as possible.

The utility knife will not cut completely through the flooring at the first stroke. Keep the straightedge in place and cut along the same score lines, being careful not to cut a ragged edge, until both the patch and the vinyl sheet flooring beneath it are completely cut through. Untape the patch sheet and pop out the newly cut patch.

Cover the marked-off worn spot in the floor with aluminum foil, shiny side up, and spread a clean rag over the foil. Using an electric iron set at moderate heat, warm the floor to soften the adhesive under the bad spot. Remove the damaged patch with a putty knife—be sure the corners are cleanly cut. Let the adhesive that is left in the patch area harden for about an hour and then scrape it completely out.

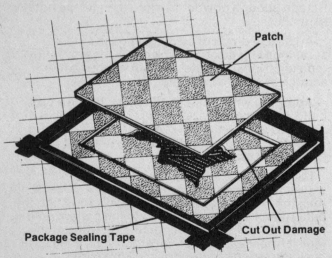

Tape scrap flooring material over the damaged area, carefully matching the pattern. Cut through patch and floor layers at the same time to obtain a patch that fits precisely.

Before you set the patch into place, make sure it fits the opening in the floor. Sand the edges of the patch slightly if necessary. Using a notched trowel, spread floor tile adhesive on the floor where the patch will go. Set the patch carefully into place in the opening, butting one edge against the surrounding flooring and then lowering the entire patch. Remove any excess adhesive.

Finally, seal the edges of the patch. Do this by covering the edges with aluminum foil, spreading a clean rag on the foil, and pressing with a hot iron. Press firmly, but don't hold the iron in one place for more than a few seconds. Remove the foil and cover the patch with a piece of scrap wood. Weight it with a can of paint or some other heavy object for the entire curing period of the adhesive. Don't wash the floor for at least a week.

REPLACING DAMAGED WOOD PARQUET

Wood parquet is beautiful, but damaged blocks can be a problem. For invisible repairs, replace the damaged wood with matching parquet tile.

To replace a damaged section of parquet, use a matching prefinished tile. If you can't get prefinished tile, finish the new tile to match before installing it. Use the whole tile or one piece of the unit, as required; replace as small an area as possible.

Remove the damaged piece of wood. If the entire tile or unit is damaged, make a row of large holes across the block, against the grain, with an electric drill or a brace and bit. Drill completely through the damaged block, but not into the subfloor under it. Then, with a sharp wood chisel and hammer, carefully split the block and pry up the pieces. Make sure you don't damage the surrounding pieces of wood.

Most parquet tile is held together with tongue-and-groove joints. At the grooved sides, carefully pull the pieces of the block out over the adjoining tongues. If the grooved sides stick, use the chisel to cut through only the top side of the groove; be careful not to damage the tongues of the abutting pieces. At the tongued sides of the tile, carefully pull out the tongue that held the damaged block to the next tile. If the tongue piece sticks, cut it off with the chisel and then carefully pry out the cut piece.

If only one piece of a parquet tile or unit is damaged, remove only that piece. With a sharp chisel and a hammer, very carefully split the damaged piece and pry out the splinters. If the pieces of the unit are held together by a wire spline,

To replace a whole tile, carefully cut off protruding bottom edges of the grooved sides with a sharp chisel and a hammer; the replacement tile will fit on top of the abutting tongues.

hold the damaged piece of wood with long-nosed pliers; cut the spline with wire cutters to free the damaged piece.

After removing the damaged piece of wood, prepare the gap for the replacement piece. Scrape the subfloor to remove any remaining adhesive; make sure all parts of the old piece of wood have been removed. If you cut a wire spline to remove the old piece, trim the cut ends flush and tap them lightly with a hammer to flatten the sharp points of the wire.

To replace the damaged wood, use a whole matching tile or one piece of a matching unit. If you're using a whole tile, match the tongue-and-grooved edges to the surrounding tiles. With a sharp chisel and a hammer, carefully cut off the protruding bottom edges of the grooved sides; the new tile will fit on top of the abutting tongues

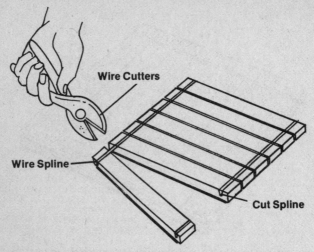

Remove the needed piece of wood from a parquet tile by cutting the wire splines that hold it in place.

instead of locking around them. Test the tile for fit to make sure you've cut enough.

If you're using one piece of a matching unit, carefully take the unit apart to remove the desired piece of wood; if necessary, cut the wire spline that holds the piece into the unit. Trim the cut ends of the spline flush, and tap them lightly with a hammer to flatten them. Test the piece of wood for fit in the gap. If the piece is too tight in the opening, sand the edges of the replacement piece lightly with medium grit sandpaper. Be careful not to damage the finish on the wood.

To complete the repair, glue the new block of wood into position. If you're replacing a whole tile, use floor tile adhesive; apply the adhesive to the subfloor in the opening with a notched spreader. On the grooved sides of the tile, apply a thin coat of wood glue to the bottom edge of the top groove. Carefully set the new tile into place, tongue sides first, to lock into the grooves of the abutting tiles; set the grooved sides firmly down over the abutting tongues.

When the tile is correctly positioned, set a block of scrap wood over it and tap it firmly down with a hammer to bond and level it. The edges of the new tile should be flush with the surface of the surrounding tiles. Quickly remove any excess adhesive with a damp cloth.

If you're replacing one strip or one piece of a unit, use epoxy cement to bond it in place. Mix the epoxy as directed by the manufacturer, and apply it to the back and to the edges of the replacement piece. Set the piece into place in the opening and tap it into place with a wood block and a hammer to bond and level it. Quickly remove any excess epoxy with a damp cloth.

To make sure that the new piece of parquet bonds firmly, cover it with a piece of scrap wood and weight it for the entire curing time of the adhesive or epoxy. Let the adhesive or epoxy dry completely before removing the weight. Finally, if the finish on the new piece of wood doesn't blend in with the surrounding floor, polish or wax the entire floor.

PATCHING HOLES IN WALLBOARD

Holes in wallboard—small or large—are easy to repair, and the finished patch will be almost invisible.

Holes less than 3 inches in diameter can be backed and filled. Remove any crumbling plaster or paper from the edges of the hole and measure it across. To make a backing, use a clean (washed in hot, soapy water) tin can lid that is at least 1½ inches bigger than the hole. Punch two holes at the center of the lid with a hammer and a nail, and thread a foot-long piece of string or wire through the holes.

Place the lid over the hole and outline its edge on the wall with a pencil. With a keyhole saw, cut a narrow slit centered on the hole in the wall, a little longer than the diameter of the tin can lid.

Choose a stick of scrap wood at least 4 inches longer than the diameter of the hole, and set it aside to use as a brace. Wet the edges of the hole and the slit with a sponge dipped in water. Mix plaster of paris according to the manufacturer's directions.

Holding both ends of the string threaded through the can lid, slide the lid carefully through the slit in the wall. Pull the ends of the string to bring the lid flat against the back of the wall. While holding the ends of the string with one hand, fill the hole and the slit with plaster of paris, smoothing plaster carefully against the tin can lid. Leave the surface of the patch indented slightly below the wall surface.

Still holding the ends of the string sticking out from the plaster, set the bracing stick over the hole, at right angles to the filled-in slit and directly between the two strings. Tie the two ends of the

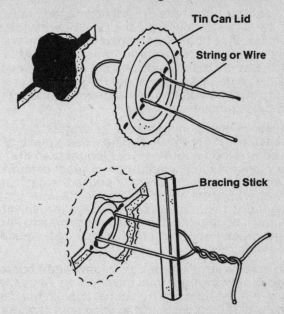

For small holes, back the opening with a tin can lid. Use wire or string and a bracing stick to hold the lid in position. Fill the opening with plaster of paris.

string firmly over the stick, pulling the knot tight so that the tin can lid inside the wall and the stick outside are both securely held. Let the patch dry for 24 hours.

When the plaster is completely dry, cut the string and remove the stick. Pull gently on one end of the string; if it comes loose, pull the string carefully out of the wall. If the string doesn't pull loose, cut the ends flush with the new plaster. Don't try to force the string or you may break the patch.

Finish the job by applying another coat of plaster of paris to level the patch. Let it dry completely and sand it smooth with fine-grit sandpaper; repeat if necessary. Prime the patched spot, let it dry for several hours, and then repaint the entire wall.

To patch a large hole or badly damaged area, cut a square or rectangular piece of wallboard slightly larger than the hole. Set this patch flat on the wall over the hole and trace carefully around it with a pencil. Set the patch aside and cut out the traced area; use a utility knife to score the paper before cutting away the damaged wallboard. Remove the sawed-out piece from the wall.

Measure the opening across its longest dimension. To back a small patch, use a piece of thin scrap wood about 4 inches longer than the hole's longest dimension. Apply contact cement to the ends of the length of wood and to the back of the wall where the brace will bridge the hole. Let the cement dry. Insert the brace sideways into the hole, position it so that the cemented areas match, and set the brace firmly in place, flat against the inside of the wall.

To brace a large patch, use a lightweight board about 6 inches longer than the opening. Slide the board into the hole and hold it flat against the inside of the wall. To hold it in place, drive countersunk screws throught the wall and into the ends of the board. Tighten the screws until the heads are below the surface of the wall.

Spread patching plaster over the exposed side of the secured brace, and cover the edges of the plasterboard patch with the compound. Set the patch carefully in place, making sure it is flush with the wall surface. Hold it in place for a few minutes while the patching plaster hardens.

Complete the job by plastering over the outlines of the patch and the exposed screw heads. Let dry completely and sand the area smooth; repeat if necessary. Prime the patched area, let dry for several hours, and repaint the entire wall.

PATCHING CRACKS IN PLASTER

Small cracks in plaster can be fixed with routine pre-painting work, but big cracks demand more drastic measures.

Large cracks must be scraped and cleaned before repairing. With the pointed end of a can opener or other suitable tool, remove loose plaster from the crack. Turn the point of the opener sideways each way to widen the opening and undercut it slightly. Vacuum the crack to remove loose plaster and dust.

Mix plaster of paris with water to a thick paste, being careful to remove all lumps. It hardens quickly, so mix only enough to fill the crack you're working on.

Paint the crack thoroughly with water, using firm brush strokes along the crack to wet the plaster inside to its full depth. Apply plaster to the crack with a putty knife or broad paint scraper, forcing plaster in to the full depth of the crack. Smooth the surface of the crack to remove excess plaster.

Let the new plaster dry completely, preferably overnight; it will turn bright white as it dries. Sand the patched area with fine-grit sandpaper to smooth and level it, then repeat the wetting and filling procedure, if necessary. Let the plaster dry again and sand it smooth. Before painting the wall, prime the patch with a light coat of paint.

Before patching a large crack in an outside wall, look for the cause of the damage. If there is a structural problem—a cracked foundation, for instance—it must be corrected before you make repairs.

Fill wide openings as described earlier. Break out any loose chunks of plaster, undercut the crack with a can opener or other suitable tool, and vacuum to remove all dust. Wet the opening thoroughly on both sides, as far in as you can reach with the paintbrush. Mix enough plaster of paris to fill the opening completely.

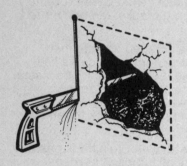

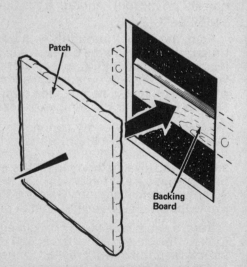

Patch

Backing Board

To brace a large patch, screw a board inside the wall, tightening the screws until the heads are countersunk.

Using a putty knife or a small trowel, fill the opening with plaster, pressing plaster all the way into the crack. Smooth the surface with a broad paint scraper. Let the plaster dry for at least 24 hours, moisten it with a wet paintbrush, and fill the crack again to level the surface. Let it dry for 24 hours, and then sand it smooth. Before painting the wall, prime the patch with a light coat of paint.

PAINTING A ROOM

Because you care more about how a finished room will look, painting a room is one job you can do better than the professionals. Thorough preparation is the key to a good paint job, and containing the mess is the way to keep the rest of your home livable during the process. Paint one room completely before beginning work on another, and keep a clean pair of shoes near the door so that you don't track paint elsewhere.

First, clear the room. Remove all drapes, carpeting or rugs, light fixture covers, and pictures. If you plan to put pictures back in the same places, leave the nails or fasteners in the walls; otherwise, remove them. Pack loose items and move as much furniture as possible out of the room. Large pieces that you plan to leave in the room should be pushed together in the middle of the room. Cover the entire floor surface, including the furniture in the middle of the room, with plastic dropcloths and spread newspapers along the baseboards. Tape the newspapers and dropcloths in place.

The walls and ceiling must be clean before painting. Scrape them to remove any loose or flaking paint, being careful not to gouge the plaster. Remove dust and cobwebs from the ceiling with a dust mop. If the old paint is very dirty, wash the walls and ceiling with household detergent or some other strong cleaning solution, using a large sponge. Let them dry completely before proceeding.

Apply masking tape to protect edges of woodwork and trim that are not to be painted. Drive in any loose nails. Remove switch cover plates and outlet covers. If you want the covers to match the walls, set them aside to be painted separately.

Loosen all light fixtures, and let them hang clear of the ceiling. Cover dangling fixtures with plastic bags. If possible, you should work by daylight; use a trouble light if you need more light.

Interior walls should be as smooth as possible. After loose paint has been removed, most small flaws can be repaired with patching plaster. Apply the compound with a putty knife, using quick, firm, even strokes to fill dents and small holes. To keep the surface even in areas where patching is extensive, use a wide paint scraper.

Long cracks need more work. Scrape along cracks with the sharp edge of the putty knife to

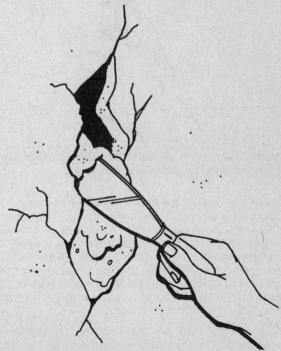

Fill wide cracks from the inside out, pressing plaster of paris in with a putty knife or trowel.

Patch small flaws in the wall with patching plaster; smooth it firmly to keep the patched surface even.

break out any loose plaster and paint chips. Vacuum the crack to remove loose material and press patching plaster into the crack with your finger, following the line of the crack. Apply more compound sparingly, using the wide scraper to cover and smooth the compound all along the crack. Fill nail holes in painted wood trim the same way, applying patching plaster with your finger and smoothing it with a putty knife.

Let the patches dry completely, preferably overnight. The compound will be bright white when it dries. Using fine-grit sandpaper and a sanding block, smooth the patched areas carefully to blend in with the surrounding wall area. The patching compound shrinks as it dries, so you will probably have to repatch large nail holes and deep cracks at least once. Follow the same procedure, sanding the new patches smooth when they are dry.

To complete your preparations, go over all wall and ceiling surfaces with a special, dry wall-cleaning sponge to remove all loose plaster dust. Vacuum the room to eliminate as much dust as possible. Finally, prime all patched areas with a light coat of paint, applied with a medium-size brush. Let the prime coat dry for several hours or overnight.

With ceiling and wall surfaces clean and smooth, you're ready to paint. Stir the paint thoroughly, following the directions on the can. Paint all corners and edges that adjoin masked trim by hand; use the tip of the brush to produce a clean edge next to a surface that isn't to be painted. Paint ceiling edges first, then wall edges and door and window frame edges. Set the brush aside, but don't clean it yet; you may need it for touch-ups.

Now pour some paint into the roller pan, filling only the deep part of the tray; clean the edge of the paint can with the stir stick as you stop pouring. Dip the roller into the paint and roll it up and down the slope of the pan to load it evenly.

Paint the ceiling first. If you have strong arms, you can use a roller extension handle or a wooden mop handle to let you reach the ceiling without a ladder, but this requires firm control. If you're doubtful, use the roller without an extension. Set up a scaffold with two stepladders and a wide plank to give you a solid footing.

You must paint the entire ceiling at one time or it will streak. Starting at one edge, apply paint to a 2- or 3-foot-wide area of ceiling, using even zigzag strokes. Fill in with cross-strokes, keeping the strokes close together. Keep the roller well loaded with paint but not dripping. Repeat this procedure across the entire ceiling, covering one area at a time and using cross-strokes to blend each area into the ones painted previously.

Use the same technique to paint the walls, working in vertical strips from left to right (if you're left-handed, you may want to work from right to left). Use cross-strokes to smooth and blend vertical strokes, and don't stop in the middle of wall. Turn the roller, if possible, to paint the horizontal strips above doors and windows.

If you want switch plates and outlet cover plates to match the new paint, place them on newspaper. Roll paint on the cover plates and let them dry. Let all new paint dry completely, and replace fixtures, switch plates, and cover plates.

Woodwork can be painted with regular flat interior paint or semigloss enamel trim paint. The semigloss is more durable and easier to keep clean.

After the paint has dried, remove all masking tape from baseboards and other trim, being careful not to mar the new paint. Stir the paint thoroughly. Paint the trim with a medium-size brush, brushing along the grain. Hold a sheet of light cardboard butted against the trim to protect the newly painted wall, painting with one hand and moving the cardboard mask with the other to keep the mask in place as you work along the trim.

Finally, paint window frames, door frames, and doors. Mask window glass with tape, and open the windows about 3 or 4 inches. After painting, move the sash to keep it from sticking. Do not forget to mask doorknobs and lock plates before painting.

Clean the brush, roller, paint pan, and other tools with cool, soapy water, and rinse them thoroughly. Fold the dropcloths paint side in.

PAPERING A ROOM

Like painting, hanging wallpaper is a skill that's easily acquired. What you may lack in expertise, you'll make up for in care.

When you buy wallpaper, figure dimensions carefully. A roll of wallpaper, whatever its width, holds about 36 square feet; of this, allowing for waste, you can use about 30 square feet. Double rolls—the way most paper is sold—are usually more economical, because they minimize waste. To figure the number of rolls of paper needed, calculate the square footage of the walls of the room to be papered, and divide by 30. Subtract one roll for every two doors or windows, but always buy at least one extra roll. Make sure the wallpaper's edges are pretrimmed.

Before starting work, remove all furniture, rugs, drapes, and pictures from the room. If you can't move large pieces of furniture out, push them together in the middle of the room. Cover the entire floor surface, including the pushed-together furniture, with plastic dropcloths, and secure the edges with masking tape at the baseboards. Remove all switch and outlet cover plates.

Before you can paper, the walls of the room must be clean and smooth. Ideally, any old paper should be removed, but if it's sound and undamaged, you can paper over it. Fill cracks and holes in painted walls with patching plaster, smoothed on with a putty knife or paint scraper. Let the patches dry and sand them smooth with fine-grit sandpaper; repeat if necessary. Vacuum the room thoroughly and go over the walls with a dry wall-cleaning sponge to remove dirt and dust. If the walls are very dirty, wash them down with a strong cleaning solution and let dry.

Sizing is used for two reasons: It makes wallpaper paste stick better, and it makes later wallpaper removal easier. Use the sizing recommended by your wallpaper dealer for use with your wallpaper and paste. Paint the walls with sizing, using a large brush instead of a roller; apply one or two coats, as recommended. Let the sizing dry completely.

With the walls patched and sized, you're ready to paper. Start at a corner and work from left to right— or, if you're left-handed, from right to left. Along the top of the wall, measure a distance about 1 inch less than the width of the wallpaper. Set a nail and drop a chalked plumb line from this point, from ceiling to floor. Snap the line to mark the edge of your first wallpaper strip.

Cut strips of wallpaper to cover an entire wall before pasting them up. Measure the wall from baseboard to ceiling to determine the length of paper that you need. Add about 4 inches to this to allow for trimming and slippage. Cover your work table with a clean plastic dropcloth and unroll the paper on it. Measure off the length needed and cut the first strip; leave it on the table, face up.

The other strips of paper for the wall must be pattern-matched to the first one. Calculate the number of strips needed. Roll out a second strip of paper on the table, matching the pattern to the first strip; you may have to waste some paper to match the strips.

Cut the second strip 4 inches longer than the measured wall height and move the first strip out of the way, leaving the second strip on the table. Repeat this matching-and-cutting process, each time moving one strip farther along the wall, until all the strips for one wall have been cut. Be sure to keep them in order. Cut short strips, still in order, as needed to work around doors and windows; make sure both the overhead and underneath strips match the surrounding paper. Cut these strips about 4 inches longer than measured as well.

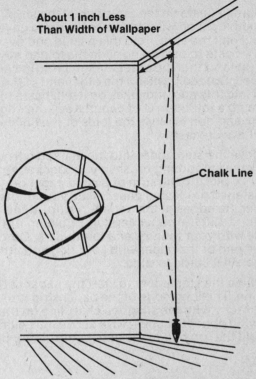

About 1 inch Less Than Width of Wallpaper

Chalk Line

Start at a corner of the room. Along the top of the wall, measure a distance of about 1 inch less than the width of the wallpaper. Set a nail and drop a chalked plumb line from this point, from ceiling to floor. Snap the chalk line to mark the edge of your first wallpaper strip.

If your wallpaper is prepasted, fill the water tray. Roll the first strip of paper loosely and set it in the water; let it soak for the recommended time before proceeding.

For unpasted papers, mix the paste, following the manufacturer's instructions. Lay the strip face down on the work table, with one end hanging over the table end.

Spread paste on the table end of the strip, smoothing it on with the paste brush, to cover about half the strip. Fold this pasted end over on itself, paste to paste, and slide the folded strip down the table so that the other end of the strip can be pasted. Spread paste on the other end of the strip and fold this end, too, back on itself, paste to paste, forming a folded-in U of paper. Keep the edges even, and don't crease the folds or the finished wall will have creases in it.

Move the stepladder into the marked corner and stick the smoothing brush in your pocket, ready to use. To pick up the strip of pasted paper or moistened prepasted paper, slide your fingers under the edges of the folded-in strip, at the center of the U. Lift the paper carefully, holding the top edge with your thumbs and forefingers. Catch the other end of the paper with your ring and little fingers if it starts to slide.

Climb the stepladder to start the paper at the ceiling. The long edge of the paper strip must line up exactly with the snapped chalk line on the wall. Leaving about 2 inches extra above the ceiling line, unfold the top half of the paper strip, lining up the

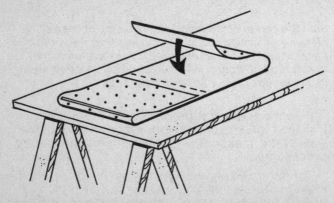

Spread paste on half the strip at a time; fold the ends over, paste side in, all edges even.

right edge on the chalk line. Smooth the paper with your hand, working back from this edge toward the corner of the room. Fold the extra inch of paper at the far side of the strip around the corner and onto the other wall.

When the top part of the wallpaper strip is securely in place, carefully unfold the rest of the strip and smooth it onto the wall, making sure it lines up exactly with the snapped chalk line. Smooth the paper slowly and firmly with the smoothing brush to remove air bubbles and excess paste, working toward the edges of the strip. The paper should now be firmly in place; if it has slid a little, correct its position with a firm pressure on the brush. A strip that's badly out of place must be peeled off and repositioned.

To secure the wallpaper around the corner and along the ceiling and the baseboard, use the edge of the smoothing brush head-on, as a pounding tool. Strike the ends of the bristles against the edges and into the corner of the wall to push the paper firmly into place. Leave the edges untrimmed until the next strip of paper is hung. Repeat this basic procedure all across the wall, making sure each new strip of paper is matched to the one before it.

To place each strip correctly, match the pattern near the top edge, set the paper against the wall next to the previous strip, and slide it to butt exactly against the already pasted paper. Correct small mistakes in placement with the smoothing brush; peel off very badly set strips and reposition them. Smooth each strip with the brush as you go.

As each new strip is set into place and smoothed, pound its top and bottom edges into place. Then trim the excess from the top and bottom of the last strip, using a sharp utility knife and following the wall-ceiling joint carefully. Replace the knife blade as soon as it begins to get dull. Press each new seam carefully with a seam roller, and wipe the roller frequently with a clean rag.

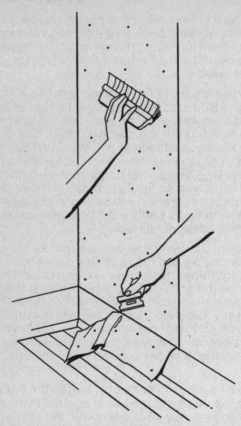

Smooth each wallpaper strip into place, pounding it firmly at the top and bottom with the smoothing brush. Then, trim the top and bottom of the strip pasted previously.

To work around a door, window, or a similar interruption, set the precut short strip into place above the opening, handling it exactly like a full-length strip. Repeat, being careful to match the pattern, with strips under windows. Trim the edges and roll the seams as before.

Use the same technique to hang paper all around

the room, matching and trimming as you go. Paper right over outlets and switches, and then go back and cut out the paper covering these areas. The switch plates will conceal any ragged edges. If a strip of paper ends exactly in a corner, fold the next strip around to overlap it slightly. Cut closely along the overlapping edge with a sharp utility knife and a steel straightedge, fold back the top layer of paper, peel off the trimmed-off strip beneath it, and restick the new edge.

Finally, when papering and trimming are complete, pick up the dropcloths and replace switch and outlet cover plates. If you have more than one complete roll of paper left over, save one roll for patching and return the rest to the dealer.

UNSTICKING A DOOR

Doors stick for a variety of reasons—anything from loose screws to the settling of the house. In most cases it's easy to unstick them.

First examine the hinges and tighten any loose screws. If a screw turns without tightening, replace it with a longer screw, or "pad" the screw hole to provide a snug fit. If you use a longer screw, make sure the head of the new screw is the same size as that of the original screw. To pad the hole, apply wood glue to the outside of a hollow fiber plug and insert it into the hole; let it dry and then reinsert the screw. Or you can dip wood toothpicks into glue and line the hole with them. Let dry, and snap the ends of the toothpicks off flush with the wood surface. Replace the screw; it should tighten securely.

If the screws that hold the hinge are tight, check the space between the door and the frame. If there's a gap between the door and the frame at the top on one side and at the bottom on the other, the door is tilted in the frame. To fix it, shim the hinge diagonally across from the binding edge of the latch side—the bottom hinge if the top swinging corner sticks, the top hinge if the bottom swinging corner sticks. Use a stepladder to reach the top hinge. If the door has three hinges, shim the affected hinge and the middle hinge.

Open the door as wide as possible and set a wedge under it to keep it in position. Loosen the screws on the door frame that hold the hinge to be shimmed; leave the screws that attach the hinge to the door in place. Cut a 1/4-inch-thick piece of cardboard to the same height and width as the hinge; cut slots in this shim to fit around the hinge screws. Slide the slotted cardboard into the hinge mortise in the door frame, slotted side toward the door and screw the hinge firmly back into place, keeping the cardboard shim aligned behind it. Close the door to see if the gap is gone and the door is unstuck. If not, cut a second shim and insert it under the hinge over the first shim.

If the door is hung evenly but has to be slammed shut, the wood has probably swollen. Examine the door to determine where it's binding. If the door is too wide, plane the hinge side of the door; do *not* plane the doorknob side. If the door is too tall, plane the end that binds, either the top or the bottom. Plane carefully, removing a thin, even strip of wood all along the binding edge; be careful not to cut too much.

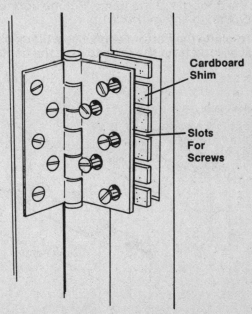

Cardboard Shim

Slots For Screws

To fix a door tilted in its frame, shim the hinge that is diagonally across from the binding edge of the latch side. Cut a 1/4-inch piece of cardboard to the height and width of the hinge; cut slots to fit around the screws.

To plane the top of a door, open the door wide and wedge it open. Working from a stepladder, plane the top of the door carefully from the edges toward the center with a block plane; don't plane from the center toward the edges or the wood will split. After planing a small amount, try to close the door; if it still sticks, plane a little more and try again. When the edge is sufficiently planed, coat the raw edge of the door with shellac, thinned according to the manufacturer's instructions. Let it dry at least 1 hour before closing the door.

To plane the bottom or the side of a door, take the door off its hinges. Remove the pin from the bottom hinge first. tapping it out with a screwdriver or a hammer; then remove the middle and top pins and lift the door out of the frame. Set the door on the floor with the hinged side up.

To plane the bottom edge, use a block plane to shave wood from the edge toward the center; then

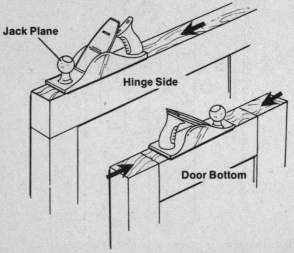

Plane the side of a door from the center of the hinged side toward each end. Plane the bottom from each edge toward the center.

flip the door onto its hinged side and plane from the other edge toward the center. Coat the raw edge of the door with shellac and let it dry at least 1 hour; then rehang the door.

To plane the side of the door, remove the hinges. With a jack plane, shave wood from the center of the hinged side to the ends; plane only a little, and be sure to cut evenly. Fit the door into the door frame to test the fit; if necessary, plane again. Shellac the raw wood of the door and let it dry at least 1 hour; then replace the hinges and rehang the door.

If neither hinge placement nor swollen wood is the problem, the door frame itself may be out of alignment; use a carpenter's square to check it. You may be able to unstick the door by adding shims or by planing; if not, turn the job over to a professional carpenter.

UNSTICKING
A WINDOW

Double-hung windows are all too prone to sticking, but you can usually open them with muscle and common sense.

First check the window to make sure it's unlocked. Assuming the catch is open, the most common problem is that the window was painted shut, and the paint is holding the sash shut. Use a stiff putty knife or paint scraper to cut the paint sealing the joint between the window sash—the sliding part—and the frame. Push the blade of the knife straight into the joint. If it won't go in with mild pressure, tap it in lightly with a hammer to break the paint all around the sash. If this was the only problem, the window should open.

If the window still doesn't open, the tracks that the sash moves in may be blocked. Examine the tracks above the sash. If they're clogged with paint or dirt, clean them carefully with an old chisel; don't dig into the wood, but remove lumps and bulges. Sand the inside of the tracks smooth with medium-grit sandpaper, then spray them with a lubricant, and raise the window.

If the grooves are clean but the window still sticks, place a 6-inch-long wood block flat against the wood of the sash frame and tap it gently with a hammer to push the sash back from the window frame. Work all around the edges of the sash with the block and hammer, tapping very gently and evenly along the sash frame; then try to open the window. If it opens, clean, sand, and lubricate the tracks. If tapping on the sash doesn't work, tap the block sideways into the window frame, to push it

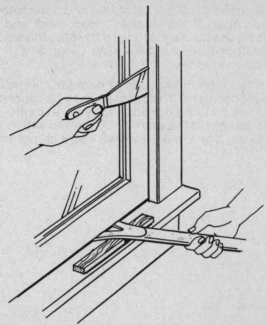

If a window is painted shut, use a stiff putty knife or paint scraper to cut the paint sealing the joint between the sash and the frame. As a last resort, use a pry bar and block of wood; pry gently under the window sash, from corners to the center.

the other way. Try the window again, and clean and lubricate it if it opens.

As a last resort, use a pry bar. Work from the outside of the window if you can. Slip the flat end of the pry bar into the joint between the bottom of the window sash and the windowsill. Set a block of wood on the windowsill under the bar to improve leverage and protect the wood. Pry gently at the corners of the window, pushing the bar down to move the window up; pry first one corner, then the other, moving slowly back and forth toward the center of the sill. Work carefully, and don't force the window open. If it does open, clean, sand, and lubricate the tracks. If it doesn't, repeat the wood block procedure from the inside. Clean and lubricate as before.

If cutting, pounding, and prying don't work, leave the window alone. The problem may be caused by excessive swelling from humidity, by extreme misalignment of the sash, or by uneven settling of the house. Don't make it worse; call a carpenter.

REPLACING BROKEN GLASS

Replacing a broken windowpane is a job you can easily do yourself.

Wearing a pair of heavy work gloves, wiggle the broken pieces of glass back and forth to loosen and remove them from the frame; if they don't come loose easily, knock the pieces out with a hammer.

With a chisel or scraper, remove all the old putty, bit by bit. Don't try to force long pieces out. Soften stubborn chunks with a propane torch or soldering iron, or paint the old putty with linseed oil, let the oil soak in, then scrape again.

If the window frame is wood, look for glazier's points (small metal triangles) as you work; in metal frames, look for spring clips. Remove them carefully and set them aside. If points or clips are missing, get some when you buy the glass.

Wire-brush the frame to remove all the traces of old putty. For a wood frame, coat the raw wood where the old putty was with linseed oil, all around the frame, and let the oil soak in completely.

Measure the inside of the frame carefully in both directions, subtracting 1/16 inch each way to allow for natural expansion and contraction and for any irregularities in glass or frame. If the lip of the frame is very wide, you can subtract as much as 1/8 inch from each dimension. Have the glass cut to size at a hardware store or lumberyard.

With the glass at hand, remove a large chunk of putty from the can. Roll the putty between your palms, shaping it into a narrow, roughly pencil-size roll. Press the putty roll around the inside of the empty window frame, starting at a corner, where the glass will be pushed into place.

Working carefully, press the new pane of glass firmly against the putty, pushing hard enough to force some of the putty out around the glass and to remove any air bubbles. Insert the spring clips (metal frame) or glazier's points (wood frame). Snap the clips back into their holes. Use the putty knife to insert glazier's points into the wood frame, pushing in the sharp points every 6 inches or so around the frame.

Before going any further, look at adjacent or nearby windowpanes. The new putty should match the putty on these panes.

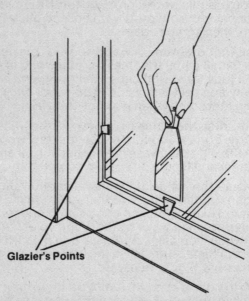

Glazier's Points

Press glazier's points into a wood frame to secure the new pane of glass. Place the points every 6 inches or so around the frame.

To apply putty to the outside of the new pane, make another putty roll. Press it firmly all around the new glass. Press hard enough so that there are no gaps.

Dip the putty knife in linseed oil and shake off the excess. Using long, even strokes, smooth the putty around the new pane. It should not be visible over the frame on the inside of the window. Use a razor blade or glass scraper to remove any excess putty, on both sides of the glass and frame.

Let the new putty cure for three days before painting it. If the surface of the putty is very rough, smooth it carefully with fine sandpaper. You don't

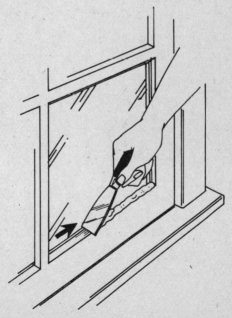

Smooth the putty into the joint around the pane with long, even strokes. Remove excess putty with a single-edge razor blade.

have to repaint the whole window frame, but let the paint overlap a little onto both frame and glass, to make sure the putty is sealed at both edges. Use two coats, and let the paint dry thoroughly before cleaning the glass.

REPLACING A BROKEN SASH CORD

You can fix a broken sash cord by using new cord, but to make this kind of repair a one-time-only effort, replace broken sash cords with sash chain.

On the side of the window with the broken cord, use a sharp razor blade or utility knife to cut the paint seal between the window frame and the inside stop molding that holds the sash in place. Being careful not to gouge the stop or the window frame, pry the stop strip away from the frame with a putty knife and remove it. The stop strip must be removed for access to either the top or the bottom sash; if you're replacing a cord in the upper sash, remove the lower sash and the parting strip—the piece of wood between the upper and lower sashes—first.

The sash cord is attached to the sash at a groove or indentation in the upper corner. Pull the side of the sash toward you out of the window frame, just far enough to expose this indentation. Pull the knotted end of the cord out of the groove, or untie the knot. Remove the cord from the sash frame and knot the end.

Lift the window carefully out of its track on the other side; you may need someone to help hold it in place. Untie the cord on that side and remove it from the sash frame, but do not release it—knot the end of the cord first, or it will slide into the wall. Remove the sash from the window frame and set it aside.

Sash cords operate on pulleys, partly visible at the sides of the window frame; the weight of the window sash is balanced by weights that hang inside the frame. To replace the sash cord, you must be able to reach these weights.

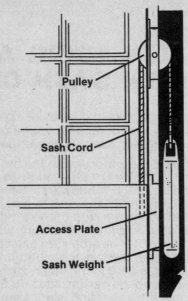

The sash cord is attached to the top of the window sash and threaded over a pulley; a weight in the frame balances the sash.

Some windows have access plates in the sides of the sash frame. Look for these plates; they may have been painted over. If you can see only a vague outline, tap the track with a hammer until the edge of the plate is clear. Cut along the edge with a razor blade or utility knife, then remove the screws in the plate and lift it out. In very old houses, there are usually no access plates. In this case, you must remove the entire inside frame of the window. Use a putty knife to pry out the sides of the frame.

Remove the weight from the inside of the frame and untie the sash cord. Using the two broken pieces of the old cord, measure the length of sash chain needed to rehang the window. Cut the chain to the correct length, allowing several extra inches so it can be looped through the sash weight and fastened.

Attach a small weight to one end of the chain—anything small enough to feed through the pulley will do. Push the weighted end of the chain in over the pulley at the top of the window frame. Feed in the chain until it is visible in the access plate at the bottom of the frame, then remove the small weight.

Now attach the sash weight to the chain. Loop the chain through the weight and bind the end to the chain with sturdy wire using pliers to pull it tight. The chain must be securely fastened or it will not hold. Replace the weight in the access hole and reel in any slack in the chain. Do not replace the access plate or inside window frame yet. Follow the same procedure to replace the sash cord on the other side with chain.

Set the window sash back into place at the edge of the window frame—you may need help again at

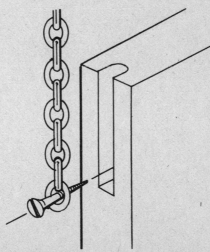

Secure the end of the sash chain to the slot in the top of the window sash. Fasten it firmly with a wood screw.

this point. Attach the chain to one side of the sash, using a wood screw to hold it in place in the slot. Lift the window sash back into its track.

Attach the chain to the other side of the sash and raise the window (bottom sash) to its highest position, bracing it against the parting stop. Check the position of the sash weight; the bottom of the weight should be about 3 inches above the sill. If the weight is not in the right place, adjust the sash chain at both sides of the sash to correct its position.

Finally, when the weights on both sides of the sash are properly placed and the sash hangs evenly, replace the access plate or inside window frame. If the window is an upper sash, replace the parting strip, the lower sash, and the stop strip; if it is a lower sash, simply replace the stop strip.

MENDING A SCREEN

A screen with a hole in it is guaranteed to attract bugs, but the repair is an easy one.

Fiberglass screen. Close tiny holes in a fiberglass screen with a dab of clear nail polish or household cement. Use only a little cement, and blot any excess immediately. Sew clean cuts together carefully with nylon thread, using a zigzag stitch over the cut edges. Don't pull the thread too tight or the mend will pucker. Seal the join with clear nail polish.

For ragged cuts or large holes, cut away any damaged screening that remains in the hole. Cut a patch of fiberglass screening to size; it should overlap the hole about 1/2 inch on all sides. Using nylon thread, sew the patch carefully into place, using a firm but not tight running stitch. Seal the edges of the patch with clear nail polish.

Metal screen. To close a pinhole in a metal screen, use an ice pick or toothpick to push the bent wires back into place. If a small opening remains, close it with a dab of household cement or clear nail polish. Apply nail polish sparingly and let dry; repeat until the opening is filled. Sew long tears together with a needle threaded with fine wire. Seal the mend with clear nail polish.

To repair large holes, cut away any damaged wires that remain in the hole. Cut a square or rectangular piece of screening about 2 inches larger all around than the hole. Pull away the outside wires on all four edges to a depth of about 1/2 inch to make a fringe of wires on each side.

Bend the fringe wires on each side over a block of scrap wood, making a sharp, even, right-angle bend

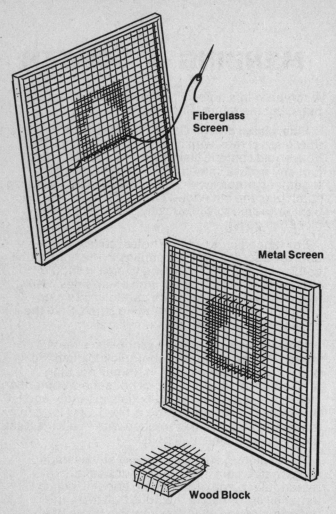

For a fiberglass screen, use nylon thread to sew the patch into place with a firm but not tight running stitch. For a metal screen, bend the fringe wires of the patch over a block of wood; place the patch over the hole and fold the fringe wires in toward the center of the patch.

all around the patch. Position the patch over the hole.

Press firmly and evenly on the patch to push the bent fringe wires through the mesh of the screen. The patch should lie flat and even against the screen. On the other side of the screen, bend the protruding fringe wires flat, folding them in toward the center of the patch. For a more secure patch, stitch around the edge of the patch with fine wire.

REPLACING DAMAGED SCREENING

When a screen has so many holes, or such big ones, that it isn't worth patching—or when metal screening becomes bulged and rusted—it's time to replace the screening entirely. As long as the frame is in good shape, this isn't as difficult as it sounds. If the frame is wood, you can use either fiberglass or fine-mesh aluminum screening; if it's aluminum, you must use aluminum screening. You may be able to buy the screening cut to size; otherwise, cut it about 1 1/2 inches larger all around than the opening. If you're working on an aluminum-framed screen, you'll also need plastic splining, a few inches longer than the diameter of the screen, to replace the old metal spline.

To replace a screen in a wood frame, use a stiff putty knife to carefully pry up the molding around the edges. Be careful not to crack the molding, and leave the brads in place to reattach it later. When the molding is off, pry out the tacks or staples that held the screening in place, and remove the screening. Pull out any staples or tacks left in the frame. If the new screening must be trimmed to fit, lay it over the frame and trace the outline of the opening on it with chalk. Then cut the screening to size, 1 1/2 inches larger all around than the traced outline.

To stretch the screening into place in the frame, you must bow or arch the frame. There are two ways to do this: by weighting or clamping. In either case, the idea is to bend the frame into a pronounced bow. To use the weight method, set the frame the long way across two sawhorses, and hang a heavy weight from a rope around the center of the frame. To clamp the frame into a bow, set it on a workbench or a wide board across two sawhorses. Place a C-clamp at the center of each long side, holding the frame to the work surface, and set a long piece of scrap wood, such as a 2 x 4, between the frame and the work surface at each end. As you tighten the C-clamps, the frame will bow over the 2 x 4's.

When the frame is securely clamped, set the screening across it, aligned along one unclamped end. Use a staple gun loaded with heavy-duty staples to attach the screening to the frame; place the staples at right angles to the frame, about two to three inches apart. If you're using fiberglass screening, turn the cut edge under about one inch before stapling it down. When the first side is securely stapled, pull the loose screening over the clamped frame, and stretch it firmly and evenly across the opposite side. Holding it firmly as you work, staple the second side into place, setting the staples two to three inches apart at right angles to the frame. Then unclamp or unweight the frame; the screening should be pulled very tight as it straightens out. Staple the other two sides into place, and trim off any excess screening. To finish the job, replace the molding to cover the stapled edges of the screening.

To replace a screen in an aluminum frame, you don't have to bow the frame, but you'll need a special splining tool to install the plastic spline. First pry up the metal spline that holds the old screening in place, using a screwdriver or a putty knife, and remove the old screening. Lay the frame flat, and position the new screening over it. Trim the edges so that the screening extends just to the outside edges of the frame. To keep the screening level with the frame, set scrap boards under it, the same thickness as the frame.

When the screening is trimmed correctly, position it so that one end and one side are lined up on the outside edge of the splining groove in the frame. Hold the screening carefully in place.

Then, with the convex roller of the splining tool, force the edge of the screening into the splining groove; be careful not to let the screening slip out of place. Secure the other two sides the same way, stretching the screening taut as you work. When all four sides of the screening are in place, cut off any excess screening with tin snips. Then, using the concave end of the splining tool, drive the plastic spline into the groove to hold the screening in place. Start installing the spline at a corner and work around the frame; where the ends meet, cut off the excess splining. With the spline in place, your screen is as good as new.

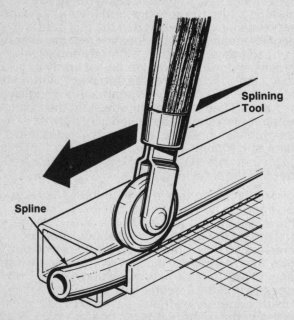

Splining Tool

Spline

In metal-framed screens, a plastic spline holds the screening in a groove. To install the screening, roll the spline into the groove with a splining tool.

REPAIRING VENETIAN BLINDS

Venetian blinds are one of the most practical and long-lasting window treatments around, but they can eventually develop problems. When the cords break or the tapes look frayed and shabby, you can give your blinds new life by installing replacement cords and tapes, often sold in kits. It's a good idea to replace both cords—the lift cord and the tilt cord—at the same time; don't install only one new cord. If you're also replacing the tapes, make sure you buy tapes for the same width slats, and with the same number of ladders, as the old ones.

If the blind is clean and otherwise in good condition, and the old cord is not broken, you can install a new lift cord without taking the blind down. With the blinds down, tilt the slats to horizontal. The ends of the cord are secured to the bottom of the bottom rail. If the bottom rail is wood, the knotted ends of the cord are simply stapled under the ends of the tapes; if it's metal, remove the end caps and the clamps from the rail to expose the knotted cords. Untie the knot on the side opposite the lift cord, and butt the end of the new cord to this end. Tape the two ends firmly together with light adhesive tape.

Pull gently on the old cord to draw the new cord up through the slats on this side, across the top, and through the control pulley; leave a loop of excess cord for the new lift cord, and then continue to draw the cord down through the slats on the lift cord side. When the taped end of the new cord reaches the bottom rail, untape the old cord and discard it; cut off any excess cord at the starting end. Knot both ends of the new cord, and secure

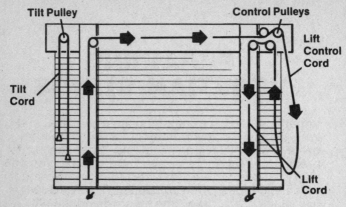

The lift cord is threaded up one side of the blind, over a pulley, across the top and through the control pulleys, and then down the other side; a loop of cord from the control pulleys forms the lift control. The tilt cord is separate.

them the same way the old cord was secured—with staples if the bottom rail is wood; with the metal clamps if it's metal. Replace the end caps on the bottom rail, and slide the equalizer clip off the old lift cord and onto the new one. Adjust the cord with the equalizer until the blind works smoothly.

This procedure takes care of the lift cord, but not the tilt cord. To replace the tilt cord, untie the knots at the ends of the cord, and remove the pulls. The tilt cord is simply threaded over a pulley and out again; it doesn't connect with the lift cord. Remove the old cord by pulling it out; thread one end of the new cord over the pulley and feed it in until it comes out over the other side of the pulley. Slip the cord pulls over the ends of the cord and knot the ends to hold the pulls on.

When the lift cord is broken, or the slats need cleaning or painting, or you want to replace the ladder tapes, you'll have to take the blind down. Lay the blind out flat, all the way open, and untie both ends of the lift cord, as above—remove the staples if the bottom rail is wood; remove the clamps if it's

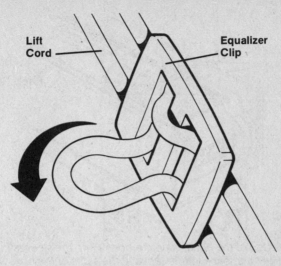

Lift
Cord

Equalizer
Clip

The equalizer clip slides onto the looped lift cord; adjust the cord on the clip.

metal. Pull the cord entirely out of the blind, and set the equalizer clip aside. Remove the blind's slats one by one, stacking them in order. If they're dirty, this is a good time to clean them; soak them in a bathtub, in a mild solution of liquid detergent, and then rinse and dry them thoroughly. The slats can also be repainted if you really want to spruce them up; use a fast-drying spray lacquer for this job.

When the slats are ready, pull out the hooks that hold the tapes in place at the top of the blind; one hook holds the tapes on each side. Position the new tapes in the top box and slide the hook into each pair of tapes, front and back, at the sides of the box. Slide the slats into place between the tapes; make sure they're all right side up, facing the right way. Fold the ends of the tapes under and fasten them to the bottom rail under the last slat.

With the slats in place, thread a new lift cord into the blind, starting at the tilt cord side and working

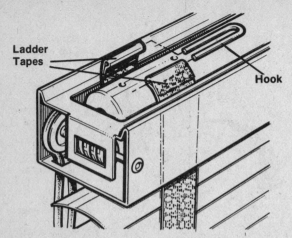

At the top of the blind, slide the hooks into the sleeves in the front and back ladder tapes at the sides of the box. One hook holds the tapes at each side.

up that side, across the top, through the control pulley, and down the other side. The tapes have woven strips—ladders—connecting the front and back pieces, on alternating sides. Insert the new cord right at the center of the tapes, so that these ladders are placed on alternate sides of the cord. At the control pulley, leave a long loop of cord for the new lift cord, and then keep threading the cord down through the slats on that side. When you reach the bottom rail, cut off any excess cord, knot both ends of the cord, and secure the ends to the bottom rail. To finish the job, slide the equalizer clip onto the lift cord and install a new tilt cord, as above.

Before you rehang the blind, check the control pulley mechanism to make sure it's working properly. If you can see dirt or lint in the pulleys, vacuum it out and wipe the mechanism clean with a soft cloth. Then spray a little silicone lubricant into the pulleys to keep them working smoothly.

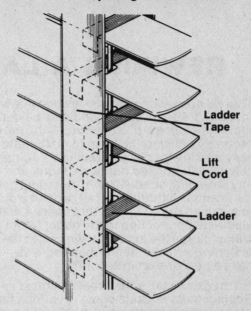

Woven strips—ladders—connect the front and back tapes.
Insert the lift cord at the center of the tapes, passing the
ladders first on one side and then on the other.

REWIRING A LAMP

There's no reason why you have to live with lamps that don't work properly, and may be dangerous too. The plug, cord, and socket—the parts that are probably causing the lamp to malfunction—are easy and inexpensive to replace. You can get them at any well-stocked hardware store, and certainly at any store that specializes in electrical parts. Why, for example, should you put up with a plug that's misshapen or broken, or that doesn't make a good electrical connection in the outlet? With a quick-clamp plug—the kind that eliminates the need for fastening wires under terminal screws—you can have a new one on in seconds.

You can install a new socket almost as easily. Replacement sockets come in various finishes— brass or nickel metal, and black or brown plastic— so you should be able to find a socket that approximates the color tone of the existing socket. And if you plan to replace a socket, why not put in a three-way socket for greater lighting versatility? Wiring a three-way socket is as simple as wiring the standard on/off version.

Lamp cord is known as Type SPT, but if you ask for zip cord at a hardware or electrical supply store, you'll get what you need. The #18 size is satisfactory for most lamp applications. Zip cord is available in many colors, the most common being black, brown, white, and transparent. Match the cord color to the lamp, and order a sufficient length for your needs. The customary length is six feet, but you can use as much cord as you need to reach from the lamp to the outlet; add the length of the cord hidden in the lamp, plus one foot for attachments to socket and plug, and for some slack. In terms of safety and appearance, it's better

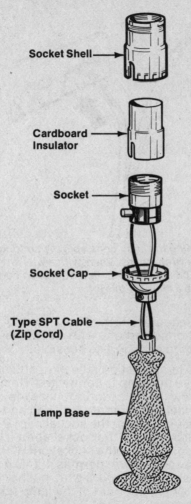

Socket Shell

Cardboard Insulator

Socket

Socket Cap

Type SPT Cable (Zip Cord)

Lamp Base

Fixing a lamp is not difficult; the electrical components are inexpensive and easy to replace. The parts that are most often responsible for lamp failure are the socket, the cord, and the plug.

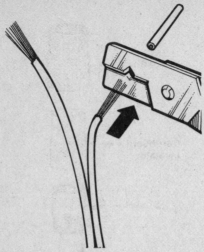

Before connecting the lamp cord, split the conductors apart for about three inches. Then, with a wire stripper, remove about 3/4 inch of insulation from each conductor end. Do not use a knife for this job.

to have an adequate length of cord than to compensate for a short one with an extension cord; but keep all cords as short as possible.

To rewire a lamp, first pull the plug out; never do any work while the lamp is connected. Remove the shade, unscrew the bulb, and squeeze the socket shell at the switch to separate the shell and the cardboard insulator from the socket cap. *Do not* use a screwdriver to pry the socket apart if you plan to reuse the socket. Pull the socket out of the shell as far as the attached wire permits. If this doesn't give you enough wire to work with, push some of the cord up from the bottom of the lamp for additional slack.

Loosen the socket's terminal screws, and remove the cord wires from under them. If the lamp is a small one and the cord goes through in a fairly straight path, you should be able to slide the old

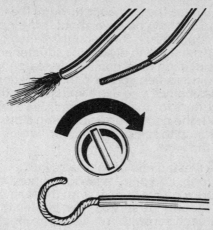

Twist the exposed conductor strands to form a solid prong (top); then loop the prong clockwise around the terminal screw. The loop is snugged in as the screw is tightened.

wire out and easily feed the new wire through from one end or the other. But if the lamp is large and the cord twists inside it, your job can be more difficult. If the old cord offers any resistance at all, don't tug on it; check to see if you can disassemble the lamp to make removal easier. Also check to see if the cord is tied in a knot to keep it from being pulled out at its base. To remove a tight cord, cut the wire off about 12 inches from the lamp's base, slit the cord's two conductors apart, and strip about an inch of insulation off the ends; do the same to one end of the new length of cord. Twist the bare new and old conductor ends together and fold the twists flat along the cord; then wrap plastic electricians' tape around the splice in as small a lump as you can, with the wrapping smooth and tapered so that it won't catch on anything. Pull on the old cord from the top of the fixture and work the new cord through; push on the new cord from the bottom at the same time to aid the process. When you have a sufficient length of new cord through at the top, clip the old cord off.

Once you pass the new cord through the lamp, split the end so that you have about three inches of separated conductors. Strip about 3/4 inch of insulation from the end of each conductor and twist the strands of each together. Be very careful not to nick the strands when you strip the insulation—a distinct possibility if you use a knife or electricians' diagonal cutters for the job. Instead, use a wire stripper with the correct size of cutting slots; this tool is designed to remove insulation without damaging the wire.

Bend the twisted end of each wire into a clockwise loop, and place each loop under a terminal screw on the socket, with the loop curled clockwise around the screw. Then tighten the screws. As each screw is tightened, the clockwise loop will pull the wire tighter under the screw head; a counterclockwise loop would tend to loosen the wire. When both screw heads are snugged firmly over the bare conductor ends, clip off any excess bare wire with your diagonal cutters. It is important that all the uninsulated wire be under the screw heads, with no loose strands or exposed bare wire. If the bare wire is visible beyond the screw heads, unscrew the terminals, remove the wires, and make the connection again.

Now slide the socket shell over the cardboard insulator, and slip shell and insulator over the socket. Then snap the shell and socket into the cap. That's all there is to it at the socket end of the lamp. A new cord, of course, requires a new plug. A quick-clamp plug is the easiest kind to connect; you merely stick the end of the cord into a slot on the side of the plug and push down on the lever at the top. Metal prongs inside the plug will bite through the cord's insulation, piercing the copper wires to make the electrical connection.

If you use a screw-type plug, however, you must prepare the wire ends just as you did when making the socket screw connections. Loop each wire around a prong of the plug before tightening the

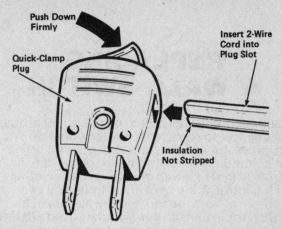

A quick-clamp plug is very easy to install. Metal prongs inside the plug bite through the cord's insulation and pierce the copper wires inside to make the electrical connection.

bare end under the screw head. The loops keep the wires apart and also make it more difficult to loosen the connections by pulling on the cord. Of course, you should never disconnect a lamp—or any other electrical device—by yanking the cord out of the wall socket, but the loops will give some strain support if the cord is jerked. Tighten the wires under the screw heads, and clip off any excess uninsulated conductor before you plug in the lamp.

REPLACING A WALL SWITCH

A malfunctioning wall switch can be a real problem, but it's simple to replace the switch yourself. You must, however, use the right type of switch. The most common type is the single-pole switch; it controls a light or a wall outlet that has no other switch control. If the light is controlled by two switches—at both the top and the bottom of a stairway, for instance—the switches used are three-way switches. Be sure you get the right type. The instructions given here are for single-pole switches only.

Caution: *Before starting to work, turn off the power to the switch; remove the fuse, or trip the circuit breaker that controls the outlet.*

With the power turned off, remove the switch's cover plate. If it has been painted over, cut carefully around the edge of the plate with a single-edge razor blade. Remove the screws and lift the plate off.

The switch is attached to the switch box with two screws. Remove these screws and pull the switch carefully out from the box, just far enough so that you can get at the wires. Now examine the wiring.

If the switch is at the end of an electrical cable, it uses a switch loop; two wires are connected to the switch, one white and one black. If the switch is somewhere in the middle of a run of cable, you'll see two cables in the box, each with a white and black wire. In this situation, a black wire from each cable is connected to two terminals on the switch, and the two white wires are connected to each other. Don't touch either of these connected white

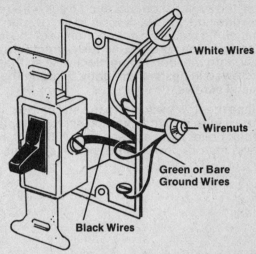

White Wires

Wirenuts

Green or Bare
Ground Wires

Black Wires

In the middle-of-the-run box, there are two sets of wires; connect the two black wires to the switch's terminals. There is no need to disconnect the white or ground wires.

wires or any bare or green ground wires that may be visible.

Now disconnect the old switch. Loosen the two terminal screws on the switch and disconnect the two wires connected to them. Discard the old switch.

Examine the new switch and you may discover that it has push-in terminals, as well as screw terminals like the old one. With these you connect the switch by stripping about 1/2 inch of insulation from the wires and pushing them into holes in the rear of the switch. To disengage the wires, you insert a narrow screwdriver blade into slots adjacent to the holes.

If the new switch has terminals only, loosen the same two terminal screws on the new switch and set the switch into the box, holding it in place. To install the switch, connect each black wire (or the one white and one black wire) to the proper terminal. To make the connections, set the loop at the end of each wire around the correct terminal screw, with the loop facing clockwise so that it can be screwed in neatly and tightly. Tighten the terminal screws.

Place the new switch into the switch box and secure it with its two mounting screws. Replace the switch's cover plate and secure it with its screws. Finally, restore power to the switch's circuit.

REPLACING AN ELECTRICAL OUTLET

An electrical outlet that doesn't work is more frustrating than no outlet at all, but it's easy to fix.

Caution: *Before starting to work, turn off the power to the outlet; either remove the proper fuse or turn the circuit breaker off at the main entrance panel or box.*

Replace the dead outlet with a new one of the same type, either ungrounded or grounded. Ungrounded outlets have slots for two-pronged plugs; grounded outlets also have holes to accept three-pronged plugs. Examine the old outlet and buy a new one of the same type to replace it.

To replace the outlet, remove the plate that covers it; unscrew the center screw and lift the plate off. If the plate has been painted over, cut carefully around it with a single-edge razor blade before removing.

Remove the two screws, one on each end, that hold the outlet in the electrical box. Carefully pull the outlet out of the box, as far as the wires inside will extend; don't force the wires out. Look at the wires carefully to see how they're connected; you must connect the new outlet exactly the same way. To remove the outlet, disconnect the wires from the terminal screws where they're attached. On an ungrounded outlet, there are two wires to disconnect, a black or red one and a white one; on a grounded (three-prong) outlet, there's also a green or bare wire. If you're not sure you can remember which wire goes where, tag the wires and their connections on the old outlet with labels made from masking tape. Lift the outlet out of the box

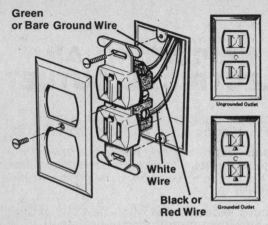

Green or Bare Ground Wire

White Wire

Black or Red Wire

Ungrounded Outlet

Grounded Outlet

An ungrounded outlet has two wires, one black or red and one white. Connect the wires to the outlet's terminal screws.

To install the new outlet, connect the wires in the box exactly as they were connected to the old outlet. One difference is that the new outlet will most likely have push-in terminals as well as screw terminals. Push-in terminals are easy to hook up: You simply strip about 1/2 inch of insulation (or straighten out the loops that wrapped around the old terminals) and push the bared wires into holes in the rear of the new outlet. Inserting a narrow-blade screw driver into slots adjacent to the holes releases the wires. Instructions on the package and on the outlet itself explain where to connect black, red, and green wires.

If your new outlet doesn't have push-in terminals, or you prefer to use the screw terminals, connect the black or red wire to the dark screw on the outlet, the white wire to the silver-colored screw. For a grounded (three-prong) outlet, connect the green or bare grounding wire to the brass or green-marked screw on the outlet and then to the electrical box. Connect each wire by looping it clockwise under the correct screw; tighten the screw firmly over the wire loop. If bare wire shows near the screw head, loosen the screw, disconnect the wire, and cut off the extra length with diagonal wire cutters; reconnect the wire.

After connecting the wires to the new outlet, set the outlet in place in the electrical box, folding the wires carefully in behind the outlet. Be careful not to pinch the wires behind the outlet. If the outlet is a grounding outlet and is set vertically in the wall, set it in with the holes for the third prongs toward the floor. Replace the two screws that hold the outlet in the box.

Finally, replace the outlet cover plate and the screw that holds it in place, and turn the power on.

FIXING A BROKEN DOORBELL

A doorbell or chime that doesn't work is no use, but usually it can be easily fixed. Doorbells operate on very little current, about 10 to 18 volts; to fix most problems, it isn't necessary to turn the power off. You may feel a tingle if you touch a bare wire, but you won't get a serious shock.

The button that rings the bell or starts the chimes is often the source of trouble. Unscrew the cover plate over the button and remove it. Gently pull the button out as far as the wires allow and loosen the two terminal screws on the back of the button; disconnect the two wires and touch the ends of the wires together. If the doorbell rings, you've located the problem—you simply need a new button. Replace the old button with a new one, connecting the wires exactly as they were before. Replace the cover plate over the button.

If the doorbell doesn't ring when you touch the bare terminal wires together, check the box that contains the bell or chimes inside the house. Remove the cover from the box, pulling it gently off the bell housing. At this point, to test the box, you'll need some help.

The box of a standard bell or buzzer has two wires connected to screw terminals. Loosen the terminal screws and disconnect the wires. Use a 12-volt circuit tester to check the wires; touch the two probes of the tester to the wires in the bell box and have someone push the doorbell button. If the bulb of the circuit tester lights, you need a new bell box.

Take the old bell box with you when you buy the new one, and buy a model that requires the same voltage as the old one. It's safe to install the box without turning the power off. Following the manufacturer's instructions, connect the new box exactly the same way the old one was connected. Replace the cover over the box.

The box of a chime assembly is more complicated, but it works on the same principle. Usually, there are three wires connected to three terminal screws—one for the front door chime, one for the back door bell or buzzer, and one for the transformer that supplies the power. Tag the wires with masking tape, marked *1, 2,* and *T* for the front door, back door, and transformer terminals. Then loosen the terminal screws and disconnect all three wires.

To test the chime box, touch the *2* and *T* wires of the box to the probes of a 12-volt circuit tester, and have your assistant push the doorbell button. If the bulb of the circuit tester lights, the chime box must be replaced. Buy a new box that requires the same voltage as the old one and connect it exactly the way the old one was connected; follow the manufacturer's instructions.

If the bulb of the circuit tester doesn't light at the bell or chime box, check the transformer that supplies power to the system. The transformer is located on a junction box or panel near the main power source, usually at the main entrance panel.

Locate the transformer, and make sure that what you're working on is the transformer. The wires from the bell or chime box are connected to terminal screws on the outside of the transformer. **Caution:** *The wires inside the junction box that the transformer is mounted on are connected to the main power lines; don't touch them! Test only the terminal screws on the outside of the transformer.* Touch the outside terminal screws of the transformer with the two probes of the 12-volt circuit tester. If the bulb in the 12-volt circuit tester lights, the problem is not in the transformer, it's somewhere in the bell's wiring system. In this case, call an electrician. If the bulb doesn't light, the

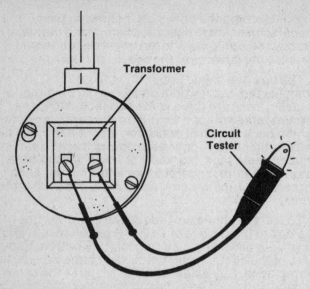

Transformer

Circuit Tester

If the 12-volt tester's bulb does not light at the bell or chime box, check the transformer. Touch only the outside terminal screws of the transformer with the probes of the tester. If the bulb lights, the problem is not in the transformer; it is somewhere in the bell's wiring system.

problem is in the transformer—either the transformer itself is defective or the power supply to the transformer is defective. The next step is to test the transformer.

Caution; *The transformer is connected to the main power system. Before working on the transformer, trip the circuit breaker or remove the fuse that supplies power to the transformer. If there's no indication which circuit or fuse this is, turn off all the power.*

With the power off, disconnect the wires from the junction box or panel to the transformer. Use a lamp socket to test the circuit that supplies power to the transformer. Attach the wires from the junction box to the screw terminals under the lamp socket and screw a light bulb into the socket. If the screw terminals are exposed, cover them with a piece of electrical tape for safety. Turn on the circuit breaker or replace the fuse that powers the transformer. If the bulb in the socket doesn't light, the circuit is not delivering power to the transformer. In this case, call an electrician.

If the bulb in the socket lights when you turn the power on, the transformer is defective, and must be replaced. **Caution:** *Before removing the transformer, trip the circuit breaker or remove the fuse that supplies power to the transformer, or turn off all the power.* Buy a replacement transformer of exactly the same capacity; install it the way the old transformer was installed, following the manufacturer's instructions. **Caution:** *Be sure the power is off before you install the new transformer.* Finally, connect the wires from the bell box to the outside terminal screws of the new transformer, and turn the power on.

CLEARING A CLOGGED DRAIN

Sluggish or completely stopped, clogged drains are no fun—but you don't necessarily need a plumber to fix them.

It's best to deal with slow-running drains before they quit entirely. Use a commercial chemical drain cleaner to improve drainage; follow the manufacturer's instructions exactly. **Caution:** *Most chemical drain cleaners are caustics. Handle them carefully, wear rubber gloves, and wash your hands and the gloves at another sink after using a chemical drain cleaner.*

When a drain clogs completely, *don't* use a chemical drain cleaner—if it doesn't work, caustics trapped in the pipes can be dangerous. In most cases, a rubber plunger can effectively remove the clog.

Use a plunger with a head big enough to cover the blocked drain opening completely. Remove the strainer or stopper from the drain and add enough water to the sink or tub to cover the head of the plunger; if the sink or tub is full, dip out excess water so that only the head of the plunger will be covered. Block overflow outlets completely with wet rags. If any other drain is connected to the same line as the blocked drain—in a double kitchen sink, for instance, or where two laundry tubs drain into one pipe—block the connected drain completely with wet rags.

Coat the bottom edge of the plunger's cup generously with petroleum jelly and set the plunger in the sink or tub, sliding it into place to cover the blocked drain completely. Pump the plunger quickly up and down 10 or 12 times, pushing firmly to build up a strong pressure; then jerk the plunger quickly away from the drain. If the clog has been removed, the water will drain out of the sink or tub. If nothing happens, repeat the plunging procedure; plunge at least twice more before resorting to more drastic means.

If repeated plunging doesn't remove a clog, use a drain-and-trap auger—otherwise known as a plumbers' snake—to break up the obstruction. Dip any water out of the sink or tub and remove the strainer or stopper from the drain. Insert the end of the auger into the drain. To feed the auger wire in, tighten the thumbscrew that locks the wire in place. Turn the handle of the auger clockwise on the wire and push to force the wire into the drain; then loosen the thumbscrew and slide the auger handle back up the wire. Repeat the procedure, tightening the thumbscrew, turning the handle clockwise, and pushing, to work the auger into the pipe.

Work the auger steadily into the pipe. If you hit a hard obstruction, the wire is probably hitting a bend in the pipe; move the auger handle right up to the drain opening and tighten the thumbscrew. Work the auger slowly into the pipe, twisting the handle to twist the wire inside the pipe, until the wire slides around the bend.

If you hit a soft obstruction, the wire has probably reached the clog in the drainpipe. Work the auger slowly into the obstruction, twisting the handle to twist the wire against the clog in the pipe. Work at the clog until you feel it break up; then twist the auger a few more times and pull the wire back, turning the handle counterclockwise to reel the wire in. Remove the auger from the drain. Flush the drain with a bucket of very hot water mixed with liquid detergent or strong household detergent.

If you can't remove an obstruction in a bathtub drain by using an auger inserted into the drain, remove the screws securing the overflow plate above the drain, and take the plate off. Insert the auger into the overflow outlet and work it down through the overflow pipe and into the drainpipe; flush with very hot, soapy water poured down the drain. If the auger still doesn't work, call a plumber.

If you can't remove an obstruction in a sink drain by using an auger inserted into the drain, tackle the clog through the U-shaped trap under the sink. Set a bucket under the trap. If there's a clean-out plug at the low point of the trap, remove the plug with pliers or an adjustable wrench. The water in the sink and the trap will run into the bucket.

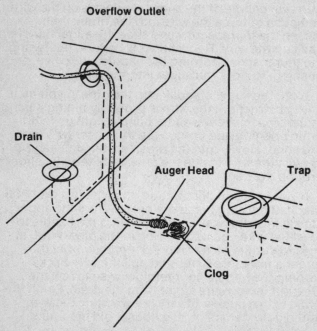

If augering through the drain doesn't work, insert the auger in the overflow outlet and work it toward the trap. After removing the clog, flush the drain with very hot, soapy water poured down the drainpipe.

Insert the auger into the clean-out opening, first up the branch of the trap toward the sink and then up the other branch toward the drainpipe. If you don't hit an obstruction in the trap, work the auger as far as you can into the drainpipe; in most cases you'll be able to clear the pipe. Pull the auger wire back and remove the auger; coat the threads of the clean-out plug with petroleum jelly and replace the plug. Flush the trap and drainpipe with very hot, soapy water.

If the sink trap doesn't have a clean-out plug, remove the entire trap. Set a bucket under the trap. Holding the trap with one hand, unscrew the slip nuts at each end of the trap section, using an adjustable wrench. Slide the nuts out of the way on the connecting pipes and carefully lift the trap out; empty it into the bucket. Check the trap for obstructions and clear it, if necessary, with the auger; then scrub it clean with hot, soapy water and a small stiff brush.

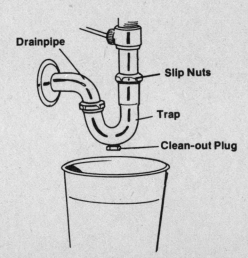

If the trap has a clean-out plug, remove it; if not, loosen the slip nuts and remove the entire trap. Set a bucket under the trap to collect the water in the trap.

If the obstruction isn't in the trap, insert the auger into the drainpipe and work it into the pipe as far as you can. If you hit an obstruction, feed and twist the auger to break it up and then pull the auger wire in; remove the auger from the drainpipe.

Finally, replace the trap. Coat the threads of the trap and the pipes with petroleum jelly and reposition the trap, being careful to replace washers and slip nuts exactly as they were before. Tighten the slip nuts that hold the trap in place. If the obstruction was in the drainpipe, flush the pipe with very hot, soapy water.

If you can't eliminate a sink clog at the trap, the obstruction may be in the main drainpipe, and may even be outside the house. Call a plumber to eliminate the clog.

FIXING A DRIPPING FAUCET

Leaky faucets waste water, burn up heating energy, and drive their owners to distraction. The repair is an easy one.

Knob-controlled faucets. Knob-controlled faucets are either separate hot and cold knobs or a single control dial, and operate by compression. Water in the supply pipes presses on a washer fitted against a U-shaped valve seat in the faucet; this pressure seals the washer against the seat and keeps the water from flowing into the faucet mouth. A drip is usually caused by a worn washer that allows leakage through the valve seat from the supply pipes. To eliminate the drip, replace the washer.

Turn off the water supply to the faucet. If there is a shutoff valve under the sink, turn it off; otherwise, turn off the main water supply. Turn on the faucet and let the water in the pipes run out. Stop up the sink with a plug so you can't lose any parts down the drain. Place a towel or a clean rag under the faucet to protect the sink's finish.

Remove the screw from the top of the handle or knob; if there is a decorative cap on top of the screw, unsnap it or pry it off with a knife, or unscrew it. If the screw won't turn, apply a drop or two of penetrating oil to loosen it; then unscrew. Remove the faucet handle.

Once the handle is off, you'll see a tall stem anchored in the packing nut that fits over the body of the faucet. Wrap a piece of adhesive or electrical tape around the packing nut and use an adjustable wrench to remove it. Then remove the stem; using

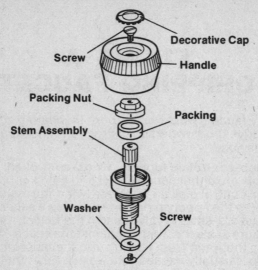

Remove the cap and the screw from the top of the handle. Then remove the packing nut and the stem assembly. The washer is at the bottom of the stem assembly, fastened by another screw.

pliers, twist it in the same direction that the faucet turns on and lift it out. The washer is on the end of the faucet stem, held in place by a screw. Remove the screw, using penetrating oil if necessary, and remove the washer from the stem.

To replace the worn washer, use a new washer of *exactly* the same size and type. Take the old washer to the hardware store and buy a duplicate. Tell the hardware dealer whether the washer is for a hot- or cold-water faucet. Also examine the screw that holds the washer to the stem; if it is damaged, buy an exact replacement when you buy the washer.

Set the new washer in place on the bottom of the stem, just as the old one was set. If the washer is beveled on one side, set it beveled side down into the faucet. Insert the washer screw and tighten it firmly. Set the stem back into the faucet, turning it in the same direction that the water turns off. Replace the packing nut and the faucet knob or handle, insert the screw that holds it in place, and tighten the screw firmly. If there was a decorative cap, replace it over the screw. Turn the water supply on.

If something other than a washer is at the end of the faucet stem, it must be replaced exactly. Some faucets use diaphragms instead of washers; pry the diaphragm off from the bottom of the stem with a screwdriver and install the new one.

Other types of faucets use rubber seat rings; hold the stem with pliers while unscrewing the center piece that holds the ring in place, then replace the ring.

If a compression-type faucet has some other device instead of a washer, either call a plumber or contact the manufacturer to get the address of a local supply store—check the Yellow Pages. Many manufacturers sell repair kits for their faucets; follow the manufacturer's instructions.

If the faucet still drips after the washer has been replaced, replace the valve seat. Shut off the water supply. Remove the handle and the packing nut, and twist out the stem. Use a seat wrench to remove the valve seat; insert the wrench into the U of the valve seat and turn it counterclockwise to unscrew the seat. Lift the seat out. Replace the valve seat with a new one identical to it; take the old seat to the hardware store to be sure you get the right kind. Install the new seat by screwing it in with the seat wrench; turn the wrench clockwise to tighten the seat firmly. Twist the stem (and washer) into place and replace the packing nut and the handle. Turn on the water supply.

Lever-type faucets. Lever-type kitchen faucets operate with a cartridge assembly, not a seat-and-washer system. These faucets rarely drip; if a lever faucet does drip, the cartridge assembly must be replaced. Contact the faucet manufacturer to find a local supply store; buy the cartridge assembly kit made specifically for your faucet. To install the new assembly, follow the manufacturer's instructions exactly.

TROUBLESHOOTING A TOILET TANK

If the water in your toilet runs constantly or you have to jiggle the handle every time it's flushed to keep it from running, the tank needs work.

Before you can fix it, you have to know how the toilet works. Take off the tank lid and set it out of the way where it won't fall and break. Look into the open tank and flush the toilet. A float ball, attached to a rod on top of the water in the tank, will sink as the water runs out; a tank ball on the bottom of the tank, shaped something like the cup of a plunger, will be raised while the water runs out and then it will drop back into place. Chances are one of these two balls is causing excess water flow.

Lift the float arm that holds the float ball. If the water stops running, the problem is in the float arm. Remove the float ball from the arm by unscrewing it counterclockwise; shake out any water that has collected in the ball and replace it on the float arm. If there was no water in the ball, bend the float arm down slightly, angling it into the tank, to lower the shutoff position of the ball. Bend the arm very gently, and be careful not to disturb its connection with the ballcock assembly at the other end. Replace the tank lid.

If the water still runs when you lift the float ball, the problem is probably in the tank ball (or flap) at the bottom of the tank. Shut off the water supply to the toilet by turning the shutoff valve, usually under the tank, firmly clockwise. Flush the toilet to empty the tank. Unscrew the tank ball from the connecting arm, turning counterclockwise. If the ball is worn or damaged, replace it with a new one of the same type. Inspect the lip of the opening the tank ball fits into; if there are mineral deposits on it, remove them with steel wool or emery cloth, or scrape them off with a knife. Make sure the tank ball or the rubber flap is firmly and properly positioned. Then replace the tank lid and turn the water on.

If the water won't shut off until you jiggle the handle, the problem is probably in the guide that directs the tank ball (or flap) ballcock assembly. Turn off the water at the shutoff and flush the toilet. Examine the valve plunger in the ballcock assembly; it's usually held in place by two thumbscrews or two pins. Loosen the thumbscrews or disconnect the pins. Lift the plunger and locate the two washers on it; a split washer wrapped around a groove near the bottom and a flat washer attached to the bottom of the plunger with a screw. Remove the split washer by prying it out with a screwdriver; remove the bottom washer by removing the screw that holds it in place. Replace both washers with identical ones; take the old ones to a hardware store and buy exact replacements. Install the washers and replace the valve plunger, tightening the two thumbscrews or reinserting the two pins. Replace the tank lid and turn the water on.

REPAIRING CERAMIC TILE

Ceramic tile is very durable, but it can eventually show signs of wear—tiles crack or loosen, and the grout between tiles wears down and crumbles out. These are more than simple cosmetic problems, because unless you repair the damage, water can seep behind the tiles and cause more serious trouble. To keep the problem from getting worse, make the repairs as soon as you can.

Replacing a Tile. The hardest part of this job, especially if your bathroom is old, is finding a tile to match the broken one. If you can't find a new tile that matches, try looking in a junkyard for an old tile. With your replacement tile at hand, remove the cracked one. The easiest way to do this, without damaging the tiles around it, is to break up the old tile. Put a piece of masking tape at the center of the tile, and drill a hole into the taped spot with an electric drill and a carbide bit. Be sure to wear safety goggles while you do this; tile chips can do a lot of damage. After drilling a hole in the tile, peel off the tape and score an X across the tile with a glass cutter. Then, still wearing safety goggles, carefully break up the tile with a cold chisel and hammer, and remove the pieces.

After removing the old tile, you'll have to clean out the gap left by it. Use a scraper or a chisel to remove old adhesive and grout from the wall where the old tile was; if chunks of plaster have been pulled out of the wall, fill the holes with spackling compound, and let the compound dry. Make sure there's no loose grout around the opening.

To attach the new tile, you'll need ceramic tile mastic, sold at hardware stores, and ceramic tile

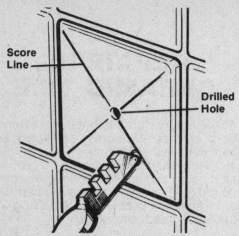

Before trying to remove a damaged ceramic tile, drill a hole through its center and score an X across it with a glass cutter. Then chisel out the pieces.

grout. Spread mastic on the back of the tile with a putty knife or a notched spreader; leave the tile edges clean. Then carefully set the new tile into the opening on the wall. Press the tile firmly in, moving it slightly from side to side to distribute the mastic, until it's flush with the surrounding tile surface. The space around the tile should be even, and the tile should be perfectly aligned. To hold it in place while the mastic dries, tape it in place with masking tape or adhesive tape; if the tile is large, wedge pieces of broken toothpick around it to keep it from slipping. Let the mastic cure as directed by the manufacturer, and keep the tile dry during this curing period.

When the mastic has cured, remove the tape or toothpicks holding the tile in place. Mix ceramic tile grout to fill the joints around the tile; follow the grout manufacturer's mixing instructions, and make sure all lumps are removed. Use a damp sponge to apply the grout all around the new tile, filling the gaps completely. Grout is caustic, so wear rubber

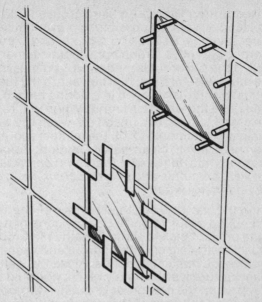

To hold the new tile in place while the mastic dries, tape it securely or wedge pieces of toothpick firmly into the open joints around it.

gloves. Let the grout set for about 15 minutes, and then wipe the wall with a clean damp sponge or towel to remove any excess grout. Be careful not to disturb the grout around the new tile. After removing the excess, let the grout dry completely, at least 12 hours—don't let the tile get wet during this drying period. Then rub the tile firmly with a damp towel to remove any remaining grout on the wall.

Loose ceramic tiles can be removed and then reattached with the same procedure. Scrape out the old grout around the loose tile with the corner of a putty knife, and then carefully pry out the tile; if it cracks, it will have to be replaced by a new one, as above. You can locate loose tiles by tapping carefully across the wall with the handle of the putty knife.

Regrouting Tile. Crumbling grout should be replaced as soon as possible to prevent mildew and water damage. Before you regrout, scrub the tile thoroughly with a strong household cleaner; rinse it well. If the old grout is mildewed, you must remove the mildew before you regrout; scrub the tile joints with a toothbrush dipped in chlorine bleach, and then rinse the wall thoroughly. When you're sure all the chlorine has been rinsed off, wash the wall again with ammonia to kill the mildew spores, and then rinse it with clean water. **Caution:** *Before you use ammonia, make sure there's no chlorine left on the wall; ammonia and chlorine combine to form a very dangerous gas.*

Let the wall dry, and then remove all the crumbling grout you can. Use the edge of a putty knife or a nut pick to scrape out the old grout., Then brush up any big chunks of grout and vacuum to remove the remaining debris. Rinse the wall again to make sure it's absolutely clean; it should be damp when the new grout is applied. Mix ceramic tile grout according to the manufacturer's instructions; make sure all lumps are removed. Apply the grout with a damp sponge, wiping it firmly over the wall to fill the joints. Wear rubber gloves while you work; grout is caustic. Smooth the newly grouted joints with a clean damp sponge; add more grout and smooth it again as necessary, to fill the tile joints completely.

When the joints are smooth and evenly filled, carefully wipe the wall clean with a damp sponge. Get the wall as clean as possible, but make sure you don't gouge the grout out of the joints, Let the grout dry for at least 12 hours; don't let the wall get wet during this period. Then scrub the wall firmly with a clean dry towel to remove any grout that's left on the tiles. Finally, to protect the new grout, seal the tile joints with a silicone tile grout spray.

FIXING A LEAKY PIPE

The best thing to do when a pipe leaks is to replace the leaky section, but that's a big job. If the leak isn't very big and the pipe is otherwise sound, you can often make the repair more simply.

To stop tiny leaks, it's easiest to use a pipe-mending cement stick, a special compound similar in form to a glue stick. This compound can stop a leak even when water is still running through the pipe, but it works best if the water supply is turned off. Turn off the water at the shutoff valve for the pipe or at the main water shutoff; drain the pipe by opening the faucet *below* the leaking section. Dry the pipe with a rag, rub the cement stick over the leak, close the open faucet, and turn the water supply on again.

To fix a minor leak in an otherwise sound pipe, use a leak repair kit or a piece of rubber cut from an inner tube. Leak repair kits usually include a rubber pad to cover the leak and a pair of curved metal plates that clamp over the pad and around the pipe; just set the pad and the plates in place and bolt the plates firmly together with an adjustable wrench.

To use an inner-tube patch, cut the patch at least 2 inches longer than the leaky area, and wide enough to wrap about halfway around the pipe. Center the patch over the leak and set a strip of scrap wood over it along the pipe; set another strip of wood on the other side of the pipe. Secure the wood strips and the patch with a C-clamp, or use one or more hose clamps; pull the clamps tight around the pipe and tighten the screws to hold them in place.

You can make a quick temporary repair to a leaky pipe with waterproof pipe-mending tape. Turn off the water supply and drain the water in the pipe by

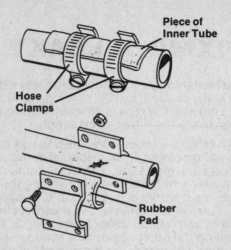

To fix a minor leak in an otherwise sound pipe, use a leak repair kit or a piece of rubber cut from an old inner tube. Leak repair kits usually include a heavy rubber pad to cover the leak and a pair of metal plates that bolt over the pad and around the pipe. An inner tube patch can be secured by one or more hose clamps.

opening the faucet *below* the leak. Dry the pipe thoroughly. Wrap the tape firmly around the leaky section, at least 3 inches beyond the leak on each side; overlap it at least half the width of the tape as you wrap. Close the open faucet and turn the water supply on; repair the pipe permanently as soon as possible.

Leaks in pipe joints are more difficult to repair. One solution is sealing the joint with plumbing epoxy paste. Turn off the water supply and drain the water in the pipe by opening the faucet *below* the leaking joint. Then dry the joint thoroughly. Apply the epoxy according to the manufacturer's instructions, being careful not to leave any gaps; cover the entire joint. Let the epoxy dry completely. Then close the faucet and turn on the water supply.

If the leak is in a large pipe or a tank, use a self-tapping plug, a specially made pipe plug that screws directly into the hole in the pipe. Although they're available in different sizes, plugs aren't recommended for small-diameter pipes because they restrict the flow of water. Simply screw the plug firmly into the hole in the pipe or tank.

STOPPING LEAKS IN BASEMENT WALLS

Water in the basement could be coming in through a weak foundation seam or through a crack in the foundation wall. Seepage all along a wall where it meets the floor can be stopped by an epoxy seal along the joint; cracks can be filled, inside and out.

To stop seepage along a floor-wall joint, use a chisel and hammer to undercut the joint. Clean all loose material from the joint with a wire brush. Mix the two parts of the epoxy mortar mix as directed by the manufacturer and fill the cleaned floor-wall joint, applying the compound firmly and smoothly with a small sharp trowel. Use the back of an old spoon to smooth the joint. Apply epoxy only when the floor is dry, and let it cure at least 24 hours.

Before filling cracks in a foundation wall, examine the outside surface of the wall. You must tuckpoint or repair cracks outside before doing inside work. Large cracks that extend well below ground level should be professionally repaired and waterproofed.

Fill small cracks as soon as outside repairs have been made. Widen and undercut the crack to a depth of 1 to 2 inches and remove all loose material with a wire brush. Mix mortar as directed. Wet the crack thoroughly; then force mortar into the undercut opening, making sure there are no gaps. Smooth the mortar level with the wall. To prevent the new mortar from drying too quickly, use a spray bottle to moisten the area several times a day for two or three days.

Open leaks and cracks that are always wet must be filled with hydraulic cement, which hardens even in flowing water. Undercut the crack or hole and remove loose material with a wire brush. Mix the cement as directed by the manufacturer. If the problem is a crack, fill the crack from the top, gradually reducing the leaking area to a hole at the bottom of the wall. To stop a leak from a hole, form hydraulic cement into a long plug, the same diameter as the hole; wear rubber gloves. Just as the cement begins to harden, force this plug into the hole in the wall and hold it in place until it is firmly set. Trowel the patch smooth.

To eliminate dampness, paint the walls of the basement with a masonry waterproofing compound

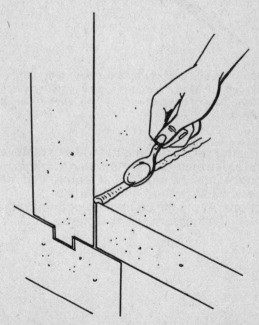

Fill floor-wall joints with epoxy mortar mix to prevent seepage. Use the back of an old spoon to smooth the joint. However, apply epoxy only when the floor is dry, and let it cure at least 24 hours.

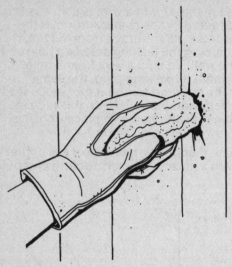

Plug open leaks and cracks that are always wet with hydraulic cement, which hardens even in flowing water. Force a long plug of cement into the hole, then trowel the patch smooth.

or paint, after wire-brushing the walls to remove dust and loose material. Some waterproofing compounds must be mixed, and require that the walls be wet; follow the manufacturer's instructions. Apply the compound or paint with a stiff brush. If necessary, use two coats.

PATCHING CONCRETE SLABS

Cracks and holes in concrete should never be ignored, because temperature changes and water penetration, especially in cold weather, can very quickly break up the sound concrete around them. To keep the damage from escalating, patch cracks and holes as soon as weather permits. Buy liquid concrete bonding agent and ready-mix sand concrete mix to repair the slab. For large or deep cracks or holes, use gravel concrete mix.

Cracks. Before a crack can be filled, it must be deepened and undercut so that the patch will bond properly. Use a cold chisel and hammer to enlarge the crack and deepen it to a depth of one to two inches. Wear safety goggles to protect your eyes as you work. Angle the chisel into the crack to make the bottom of the opening wider than the top; this will lock the patch concrete into the gap. Then remove all chunks of concrete, and brush the remaining debris out of the crack with a stiff broom or whisk broom. Flush the cleaned crack thoroughly with a garden hose, turned on full-force, and then sponge out any standing water. If the crack goes all the way through the slab, and ground underneath is eroded, pour sand into the crack just to the bottom edge of the slab. Dampen the sand thoroughly with the hose.

While the crack is still wet, mix the concrete as directed. A sturdy wheelbarrow is the most convenient container; use a shovel to mix the concrete. When the concrete is mixed, pour liquid concrete bonding agent into the crack to coat the inside surface entirely. Spread the bonding agent with a stiff paintbrush, and clean the paintbrush

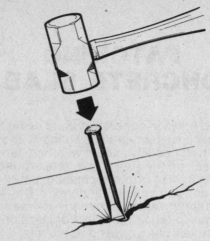

Enlarge and deepen the crack with a cold chisel; angle the chisel out to undercut the crack.

immediately when you finish. Then quickly fill the crack with the wet concrete. Pack the concrete in with a trowel, and make sure there are no air spaces along the bottom of the crack. Smooth the concrete along the surface of the crack with the trowel. If the crack is very wide, the surface of the patch should be leveled with the surrounding surface. Set a piece of 2 x 4 on edge across one end of the crack, and pull the 2 x 4 in zigzags along the entire length of the crack. This will level the patch and remove excess concrete.

Let the concrete set for about 45 minutes. When the sheen of water has disappeared from the surface, smooth the concrete again with a steel finishing trowel or a clean piece of 2 x 4—a trowel will give the concrete a denser, more polished finish. Then let the concrete cure for about a week. During this time, spray the crack two or three times a day with the hose to keep the concrete from drying out too quickly. If the crack is very wide, cover it with a sheet of plastic during the curing period. Lift the plastic two or three times a day to spray the crack.

Holes. Before you can fill the hole, you must undercut it; if it's shallow, it must be deepened to at least one inch. Remove all loose concrete. Then, wearing safety goggles to protect your eyes, deepen the hole with a cold chisel and hammer. Cut all the way down to sound concrete, and angle the chisel out at the edges so that the bottom of the hole is wider than the top. Remove the broken concrete and sweep out the debris with a stiff broom or whisk broom; then flush the hole thoroughly with a garden hose, turned on full-force. Sponge out any standing water left in the hole. If the hole extends all the way through the slab, and the ground underneath is eroded, pour sand into the hole to the bottom edge of the slab, and moisten the sand thoroughly.

While the hole is still wet, mix the concrete in a wheelbarrow, as directed. Then quickly cover the

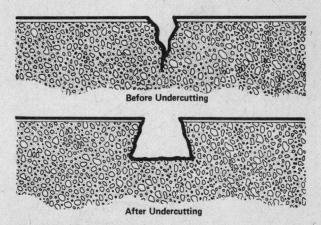

Before Undercutting

After Undercutting

A crack that isn't enlarged (top) is wider at the top than at the bottom. A correctly undercut crack (bottom) is wider at the bottom than at the top. The patch concrete is locked into the opening.

inside surface of the hole with the concrete
bonding agent. Spread the bonding agent with a
stiff paintbrush; pay particular attention to the
undercut edges. Clean the paintbrush immediately.
As soon as you've spread the bonding agent, shovel
the new concrete into the hole; pack it into the
undercut edges with a trowel. Mound the concrete
slightly above the surface of the slab, and then
pound it down with the back of the shovel. Cut
through the concrete slightly above the surface of
the slab, and then pound it down with the back of
the shovel. Cut through the concrete with the blade
of the shovel to make sure there are no air spaces,
and then pound the patch down again. Leave the
new concrete slightly higher than the surrounding
surface.

Use a piece of 2 x 4 to level the patch. You can do
this by yourself if the patch is small; you'll need a
helper to level a large patch. Set the 2 x 4 across the

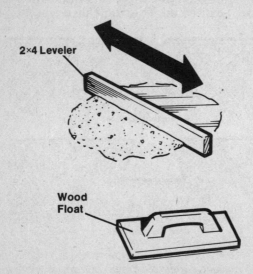

2×4 Leveler

**Wood
Float**

*Pull a piece of 2 x 4 across the patch in zigzags to remove
excess concrete and level the surface. Smooth the new
concrete with a wood float.*

filled hole, and pull it in zigzags over the new concrete; the 2 x 4 will remove the excess and bring the concrete level with the surrounding surface. The new concrete will have a sheen of water on the surface. Let it set for about 45 minutes to an hour, and then, when the surface water has disappeared, smooth the concrete with a wood float until the surface is filmed with water again. Use long, smooth strokes and press lightly so you don't mark the new concrete; stop smoothing as soon as the water sheen reappears.

Let the concrete set again until the water sheen has disappeared. If you want a rougher, nonskid texture, finish the surface of the patch with a push broom. Set the broom on the old concrete to one side of the patch, and then push it slowly and evenly across the patch and onto the old concrete on the other side. Don't push the broom hard enough to dig into the concrete; what you want is an even brushed look. After this final texturing, let the concrete cure for at least a week. To keep it from drying out too quickly, cover the patch with a sheet of plastic. Two or three times a day during the curing period, remove the plastic and spray the patch lightly with the hose.

REPLACING A BRICK

A loose or broken brick in a wall or chimney looks bad, and it can lead to further damage. But the repair is an easy one.

Wearing safety goggles, use a cold chisel and a sledgehammer to remove the mortar around a loose brick, working carefully to avoid damaging the loose brick or surrounding bricks. Lift the loosened brick out from the wall or chimney and set it in a bucket of water to soak.

If a loose brick cannot be easily removed, or if the brick is broken, break it up to remove it. Wearing safety goggles, chop out the damaged brick with a wide brick chisel and a sledgehammer, being careful not to damage surrounding bricks. Fill a bucket with water and set a replacement brick in it to soak.

Still wearing safety goggles, remove all remaining mortar from the hole left by the brick; use the sledgehammer and cold chisel to remove large chunks of old mortar, and then wire-brush the cavity to remove any debris still adhering to the bricks. Flush the cavity thoroughly with a garden hose.

Mix a small batch of mortar according to the directions on the package. To see what color the mortar will be when it dries, spread a little mortar on a scrap piece of corrugated cardboard; as the cardboard absorbs water from the mortar, the mortar's color will lighten. Add mortar coloring as necessary, experimenting with mortar applied to the cardboard until the new mortar matches the old. Mix enough mortar to replace the brick and add coloring in the proportion used in the test batch.

Before replacing the brick in the wall, spray the

wall cavity again with the garden hose to dampen it; the cavity should be wet but not streaming. Spread a thick bed of mortar on the bottom surface of the cavity, smoothing it roughly level.

Remove the replacement brick—salvaged or new—from the bucket of water and shake it to remove excess water. Apply mortar generously to the top and ends of the brick; don't, however, mortar the back. Set the brick carefully into place in the prepared hole, pressing it in firmly. It should align with the bricks on each side of it; adjust it to match, applying more mortar as necessary. Make sure the face of the new brick is flush with the surface of the wall.

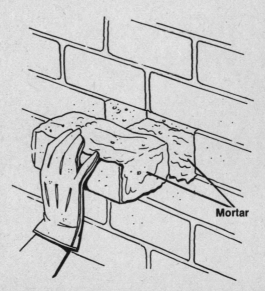

Mortar

Before installing the replacement brick, wet the cavity in the wall and spread a thick bed of mortar on the bottom surface only, smoothing it roughly level. Apply mortar generously to the top and ends of the brick; do not, however, mortar the back. Set the brick carefully into place in the prepared hole, pressing it in firmly.

When the new brick is firmly in place, force mortar into the top and side joints of the brick to fill them completely. Smooth the mortar all around the new brick, making sure there are no gaps. Scrape excess mortar from the wall with the side of the trowel. Then, using the trowel, a brick jointer, or a thin metal rod bent to form a handle, tool the new mortar joints to match the joints in the rest of the wall.

To keep the new mortar from drying too quickly, spray it lightly with the garden hose several times a day for two or three days. When the mortar has set completely, use a stiff scrub brush to remove any excess mortar from the face of the wall.

CAULKING CRACKS
AND CREVICES

No matter how well your home is built, it must also
be well caulked if it is to function properly.
Caulking serves three important purposes: it
finishes the joints where outside surfaces meet; it
prevents drafts and heat loss; and it prevents water,
dirt, and insects from entering and damaging your
home. Caulking is important everywhere two
outside surfaces meet. To make sure your home is
sealed against the elements, you should inspect it
yearly for missing or damaged caulking, and
recaulk as necessary to repair the damage.

There are several types of caulking compound.
Oil-base caulks are the least expensive, but also the
least durable; for most applications, acrylic latex or
silicone caulk is better. Acrylic latex, an all-purpose
caulk, can be painted over. Silicone caulk is far
more durable, and is very easy to work with, but it's
also very expensive, and it usually can't be painted
over. For masonry-metal joints—where pipes go
through the foundation wall, for instance—use
butyl rubber caulk. Polyvinyl acetate (PVA) caulk is
also available, but it's less durable and less widely
used than other types. For caulking wall-to-roof or
chimney-to-roof joints, use roofing compound. All
of these types of caulk are sold in bulk tubes, to be
used with an inexpensive caulking gun. Many
caulks are available in white, gray, black, and clear
forms. When you buy caulking compound, read the
label to estimate how much you'll need; it's a good
idea to buy one or two tubes extra.

Plan routine caulking for dry, warm weather;
caulking should not be done when it's very cold or
very hot. If you must work in very cold weather,
warm the caulk to room temperature before you

start. If you must work in very hot weather, chill the caulk briefly in the refrigerator to keep it from getting runny. All surfaces should be dry when you apply caulking compound.

Caulking is not a difficult procedure; all it really requires is patience and attention to detail. When you're ready to work, inspect your home carefully to find the places that need caulking. In general, there should be caulking along every joint where two outside surfaces meet—around windows and doors, at the point where the house walls meet the foundation, where porches or steps are attached, around air conditioners, pipes, and vents. Every corner seam should be caulked, and every seam between sheets of siding. On the roof, there should be caulking where the chimney meets the roof and along every flashing edge, at the chimney surface and at the roof surface. If caulking is missing or damaged at any of these points, you should recaulk the entire joint.

Before you can apply new caulk to a joint, you must remove the old caulking. Sometimes you can peel the old caulk out in long strips. If you can't, and if it's hard to dislodge the caulk with a putty knife, use a sharp utility knife to cut the old caulk out, forming a clean, square joint. Be careful not to damage the joint surfaces. For joints along glass, carefully scrape the glass with a single-edge razor blade or a glass scraper, and then clean and dry the glass. After removing the old caulk, go over the joint with a dry paintbrush to remove dust and other debris.

Once you get the feel of it, caulking is very simple. With a sharp utility knife, cut off the tip of the caulk tube's nozzle, cutting at an angle. Most tubes have cutting guidelines marked on the nozzle. The open tip of the nozzle should be roughly the same diameter as the width of the narrowest cracks to be caulked; the bead of caulk must be wide enough to overlap both sides of the joint. For larger cracks or joints, you'll have to recut the nozzle to make a wider bead of caulk. With the nozzle cut to correct width, pull out the plunger of the caulking gun and set the tube of caulk into the gun, base first, so that the nozzle of the tube sticks out through the slot on the end of the gun. Then turn the plunger of the gun to point up, and push it in just until it engages. Finally, break the seal between the tube and the nozzle; push a piece of stiff wire or a long nail into the nozzle to puncture the foil or plastic seal.

To use the caulking gun, hold the nozzle at a 45-degree angle to the joint you want to fill. With the plunger of the gun engaged and the seal of the tube broken, squeeze the handle firmly. In a few moments, caulk will begin to flow out of the nozzle. The caulk is forced out of the tube by the pressure of the plunger; as you squeeze the handle of the gun, the plunger moves in, notch by notch, and the caulk flows out. Draw the nozzle of the tube slowly along the open joint, with the tip slanted in the direction you're caulking. The caulk should flow out behind the nozzle as you go; don't try to push it ahead of the nozzle. As you work with the caulking gun, let the caulk flow at its own rate; don't try to hurry it. The gun releases caulking compound at a steady rate, one click at a time. You can't speed it

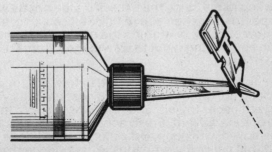

Cut off the tip of the caulk tube at an angle, to the width of the narrowest joint to be filled. Most tubes are marked with cutting guidelines.

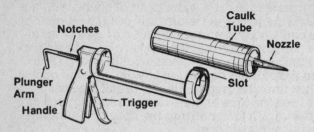

To use a caulking gun, pull out the plunger arm to disengage the notches, and insert a tube of caulk, base first, so that the nozzle sticks out through the slot at the end of the gun. Turn the plunger arm and push it in to engage it. To apply the caulk, squeeze the trigger.

up by squeezing the handle harder—All you can do is adjust your rate of movement to use it well.

Fill each joint with one steady movement from end to end, adjusting your speed as necessary to the flow of caulk. The caulk should fill the joint completely, overlapping both side surfaces, with no gaps or bubbles. At the end of the joint, twist the nozzle out and turn the gun nozzle up to minimize the flow of caulk. Don't expect it to stop flowing instantly; the caulk released by the last click will keep coming. If caulk builds up on the nozzle between joints, wipe the excess off the nozzle with a paper towel. When you're finished caulking, stop the flow of caulk by turning the plunger to point down and pulling it out to disengage it from the tube of caulk.

Let the caulk cure as directed before you touch it. To clean up, remove as much excess caulk as you can with paper towels, and finish the job with the appropriate solvent. Fresh acrylic latex caulk can be removed with soap and water; dried silicone caulk will peel off your hands like rubber cement. Use leftover caulk as soon as possible; it will eventually harden in the tube.

Fill each joint smoothly and evenly; the caulk should overlap both surfaces, with no gaps or bubbles. Hold the gun so the caulk flows behind the nozzle.

REPLACING DAMAGED SIDING

When clapboards or shakes are rotten or broken, your home's siding can no longer do the job it's meant to do. Damaged siding lets air, water, dirt, and insects through to the inside; at the same time, it leads to decay and further damage in the wood around it. When you notice a bad spot in your home's siding, repair it as soon as you can—the damaged board or shake is the only part that must be replaced, and the job goes fairly quickly. Replace the old board with a new one of the same size and shape.

Clapboards. To remove the damaged board, you'll have to wedge it away from the house. Drive wedges up under the damaged board to pull it out from the sheathing below it. Look for the nails in this section of clapboard, and pull them out. If you can't remove them with a claw hammer or pliers, cut them off flush with the sheathing with a hacksaw. To release the top of the board, drive wedges under the clapboard that overlaps the damaged board, and remove the nails from the top of the board.

Once the siding has been released, you can cut the damaged section out. Leave the wedges in place under the clapboard. Cut through the board on each side of the damaged area, using a backsaw or a hacksaw. If you don't have enough room to use a saw conveniently, use a hacksaw blade with one end wrapped with electrical tape. Cut all the way through the board to bracket the damaged area; if necessary, move the wedges to make room for the saw. When the board is completely cut through on both sides of the damage, the damaged section should pull down and out fairly easily. If it won't come out, break it up with a hammer and chisel,

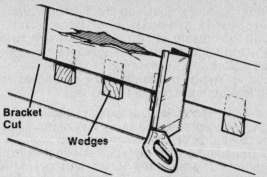

To remove a damaged clapboard, drive wedges to pull it away from the house, and pry out the nails. Then cut out the damaged section with a backsaw.

and remove it in pieces. Be careful not to damage the surrounding boards.

Cut the new clapboard to fit the opening, and test it for fit; it should slide right into place, with its top edge under the board above and its bottom edge over the board below. Plane the edges for an exact fit, if necessary. When the new board fits well, paint it with a primer coat; make sure both sides and all edges are covered. Also paint the raw edges of the opening, where the old siding was cut out. Let the paint dry completely. Then set the new board into

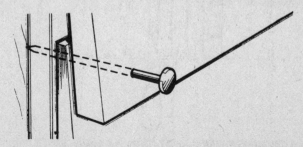

Slide the new clapboard into the gap, with its top edge under the board above and its bottom edge over the board below.

the opening, and adjust it so that it fits perfectly.
Nail the board into place with 16d nails, driven
through the bottom and through the board above
into the top edge. Caulk the edges of the patch with
acrylic latex caulk, as detailed previously in
"Caulking." When the caulk is dry, paint the new
siding to match the rest of the house.

Shakes or Shingles. Damaged shakes or
shingles are replaced the same way clapboards are.
If they're natural unstained cedar, however, it's a
good idea to take your replacement shakes from an
inconspicuous area of the house, and to use the
new shingles on that spot. This trick eliminates a
new-looking unweathered patch in the repair area.

Wedge each damaged shake or shingle out,
driving wedges under the damaged shake and
under the shakes that overlap it. Pull out or cut off
all nails, as above. Then remove the damaged shake.
If it doesn't come out easily, split it into several
pieces with a hammer and chisel, and remove the
pieces. Insert the new shake and nail it into place
with 16d aluminum nails; do not use steel nails. If
the shake doesn't have predrilled nail holes, drill
pilot holes for the nails to keep the wood from
splitting.

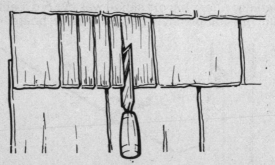

*If a damaged shake doesn't come out easily, split it into
several pieces with a hammer and chisel; remove the pieces
and pull out the nails.*

FIXING A
LEAKY ROOF

The hardest part of fixing a leaky roof is finding the leak; once that's done, the job is easy.

You can't fix the roof while it's wet, but try to locate the leak while it's raining. If the leaky roof is above an unfinished attic or crawl space, climb into the attic. Shine a flashlight along all the beams in the general area of the leak to see where the water comes in; watch for the shine of the water in the light. In daylight, examine the roof for wet spots and discolored patches. Water coming in through a pitched roof usually runs down the beams before dripping through into the rooms below, so trace every wet spot or stream of water back to its source.

When you've located the leak, mark it. On the inside, draw a circle around the bad spot with chalk. If you can, force a stiff wire up through the roof deck until you feel it push through to the outside. The wire will flag the leak outside so you can spot it when you can do the repair work.

If the attic is finished, you can only make an educated guess as to where the leak is. Draw a rough plan of the roof above the leaky area, and mark chimneys, dormers, vent pipes, ridges, valleys, and flashing on the sketch. These are all potential trouble spots; any such situation anywhere near the leak inside might be the source of the problem outside.

When the rain has stopped and the roof has dried out completely, assemble your tools and set up an extension ladder to give you access to the roof. **Caution:** *Make sure the ladder is firmly braced against the house; the top of the ladder should stick* up above the edge of the roof. Wear old clothes and rubber-soled shoes.

Asbestos shingle roofs. In the leak area, look for missing or torn shingles, curled-up shingles, or— around the chimney or some other interruption— breaks in flashing joints or gaps in joints finished with roofing compound. If you can't find any evidence of damage, call a professional.

To refasten a curled-back shingle, gently straighten the edges of the shingle. This is easy in hot weather; in cold weather you may have to soften the shingle first. To soften a brittle shingle, carefully place the diffused flame of a propane torch over the curled edges. Apply only enough heat to soften the shingle, not enough to ignite it. Apply roofing compound generously to the bottom of the loose shingle with a putty knife and press the shingle firmly into place.

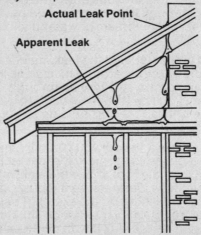

Try to locate a leak while it is raining. If the leaky roof is above an unfinished attic or crawl space, climb into the attic. Shine a flashlight along all the beams to see where the water comes in. Water coming in through a pitched roof usually runs down the beams before dripping through into rooms below, so trace every wet spot or stream of water back to its source.

To replace a torn or rotten shingle, remove it carefully from the roof. Lift the edges of the shingles that overlap the damaged one and carefully pry out the nails that hold the damaged one in place; use a pry bar. Slide the old shingle out from the surrounding ones and scrape out any roofing compound left in the opening.

If possible, replace damaged or missing shingles with matching shingles, saved from the original installation. If you don't have any of the original shingles and can't get shingles that match, use nonmatching shingles or cut shingle-size patches from sheet copper or aluminum. They won't look as good, but they'll do the job.

Round the back corners of the replacement shingle slightly with a sharp utility knife or, for sheet metal, tin snips. Slide the shingle into place, its front edge aligned with the other shingles in the row, its back edge under the overlapping shingles in the next row up. If you're using a sheet metal patch, apply roofing compound to the back of the patch before sliding it into place.

Nail the new shingle into place under the overlapping edges of the shingles above it. Gently lift the overlapping corners. Drive a roofing nail through each top corner of the new shingle and cover the head of each nail with a dab of roofing compound. Smooth the lifted edges of the overlapping shingle into place.

Follow the same procedure to replace rows of shingles. To replace ridge shingles, use the same technique, but before nailing the new shingle into place, coat the back of the shingle with roofing compound. Nail the corners into place and cover the heads of the nails with roofing compound.

Examine flashing, valleys, and coated vent pipes for damage. If the metal flashing around a chimney or dormer is pulling loose from the mortar that holds it, it must be replaced; otherwise, apply roofing compound to questionable areas with a putty knife or small trowel. Cover any exposed nails with roofing compound. Clean up with mineral spirits and rags.

Flat roofs. Damage to flat roofs is usually easy to see. Look for blisters of roofing felt that have cracked. Cut the blister open with a sharp utility knife, being careful to cut only the blistered layer of felt. Lift the sliced edges back from the middle of the blistered spot. If there's water inside, press the surrounding area to force it out to the top; then use a propane torch, very carefully, to dry the inside of the blister. If the day is dry and sunny, let the blister dry naturally.

Apply roofing compound to the bottom edges of the loose flaps and press them down firmly. Nail the cut edges down with roofing nails and coat the entire blister with roofing compound. Cut a patch of 15# roofing felt to cover the blister area. Set it into place and nail it down with roofing nails, spacing nails 1/2 inch apart around the edges of the patch. Coat the entire patch with roofing compound, making sure the heads of the nails are well covered.

To repair a hole in a flat roof, measure and mark an even patch around the hole. Cut out the damaged area carefully with a sharp utility knife, keeping the edges of the cut even. If the hole is a deep one, work through one layer of roofing felt at a time, cutting out and removing each layer that is visibly damaged. Remove all damaged layers, but don't cut deeper than you have to. Let the cutout area dry thoroughly or, if necessary, dry it very carefully with a propane torch.

Cut a patch of 15# roofing felt to replace each damaged layer of felt you've removed. Cut patches carefully to fit the hole. Apply roofing compound to the bottom of the hole and set a roofing felt patch into the hole; coat the top of the patch with roofing compound. Repeat to replace each cutout layer of roofing felt.

Coat the top patch layer with roofing compound, extending the compound 2 inches past the patch on all sides. To seal the repair, cut another patch 4 inches longer and wider than the filled-in hole. Set this patch carefully onto the surface of the roof over the patch and nail it into place, spacing roofing nails 1/2 inch apart around its edges. Finally, coat the heads of the nails with roofing compound.

Examine joints and flashings for damage and apply roofing compound to questionable areas. Cover any exposed nails with roofing compound. If the entire flat roof surface is badly worn, and you can see many worn spots or fine cracks, coat the entire roof with liquid roofing compound. Spread the compound with a large stiff brush or a broom— you'll have to throw away the brush or broom, so don't use a good one. Clean up with mineral spirits and rags.

Wood shake or shingle roofs. Replace split shingles or shakes with new ones of the same type; replace ridge shingles with specially mitered shingles. To remove the damaged shingle, split it carefully with a sharp wood chisel and a hammer, holding the chisel up into the shingle at the slant of the roof and being careful not to damage the surrounding shingles. Pull the broken pieces of the old shingle out of the roof.

Measure the opening to be filled and cut a new shingle 3/8 inch narrower with a fine-toothed handsaw. Before setting the shingle into place, cut off the nails that held the old shingle. Slide the blade of a hacksaw carefully under the overlapping shingles and saw off the heads of the nails, cutting as far down the nail shaft as you can.

Slide the new shingle into place, under the overlapping shingles and over the sawed-off nails. Secure it in position with two roofing nails, one on each edge of the shingle that's covered by the overlapping shingles above it. Set the heads of the nails with a nail set and cover them with roofing compound. Replace each damaged shingle the same way.

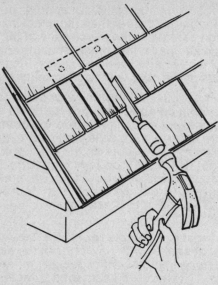

To remove a damaged shingle, split it carefully with a sharp wood chisel and a hammer, holding the chisel up into the shingle at the slant to the roof and being careful not to damage the surrounding shingles. Pull the broken pieces of the old shingle out of the roof.

MAINTAINING GUTTERS AND DOWNSPOUTS

Clean gutters regularly to keep them working properly; repair damaged sections at the same time. Gutters should be cleaned at least twice a year, in late spring and late fall; more frequent cleaning is advisable if you live in a wooded area. Set an extension ladder against the house, bracing it firmly so that the top of the ladder sticks up above the edge of the roof. Wear old clothes and rubber-soled shoes.

Wearing work gloves, clean leaves and debris from the gutters with a plastic scoop. **Caution:** *Move the ladder frequently; don't try to reach too far along the gutter from any one position.* Flush any remaining debris from the gutter with a garden hose.

If downspouts are clogged, use a plumbers' snake to break up the obstruction; flush the spout with a garden hose. To prevent clogs from forming, insert a wire leaf strainer into each downspout, just far enough to set it firmly into place. Use copper leaf strainers for copper gutters, stainless steel for other types.

You'll probably be tempted to buy plastic or wire-mesh leaf guards to set over the length of the gutter—don't do it. Screening-type leaf guards don't eliminate the need for regular gutter cleaning, but they often discourage it.

Let the gutters dry and then patch holes and rust spots. Wire-brush the damaged area to remove loose rust and paint; clean the wire-brushed area thoroughly with a rag and mineral spirits.

To repair minor damage, apply roofing compound to the damaged area with a putty knife. To repair larger holes, cut a patch of wire screening about 2 inches longer each way than the hole or crack. Apply roofing compound generously to the damaged area; press the screening patch into the compound and coat it with another generous layer of roofing compound. Let dry; if necessary, apply more roofing compound to completely seal the patch.

Patch extensively damaged sections with sheet metal—copper for copper gutters, aluminum for other types. Cut a patch of sheet metal with tin snips, roughly large enough to line the inside of the gutter completely over the damaged area and fold back over the outside lip of the gutter, at least 1 inch longer than the hole each way. Set the rough-cut patch into the gutter and bend it to fit exactly over the damaged area; remove it and trim the edges as necessary.

Coat the inside of the gutter generously with roofing compound where the patch will cover it. Press the patch into place over the roofing compound, smoothing it tightly into the corners of the gutter. Bend the outside edge of the patch with pliers to clamp it over the lip of the gutter. Coat the patch generously with roofing compound, making sure all edges inside the gutter are covered. Clean tools with mineral spirits and rags.

Where the gutter sags, it isn't being adequately supported. Reset gutter hangers at sagging spots; adjust or renail sleeve-and-spike supports; renail loose fascia brackets or strap hangers with 6-penny galvanized roofing nails. Cover strap hanger nails with roofing compound. If necessary, add new hangers to correct sag, spacing hangers about 2-1/2 feet apart. Use either sleeve-and-spike or strap hangers; cover strap hanger nails with roofing compound.

Reattach any loose sections of downspout or elbow. For a temporary repair, use duct tape, but

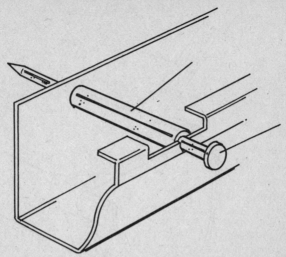

The sleeve-and-spike support is nailed to the fascia to hold the gutter in place.

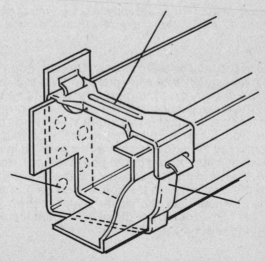

The fascia bracket is attached to the fascia; an arm clamps over the gutter.

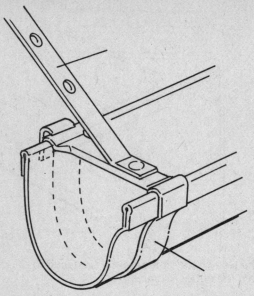

The strap hanger wraps around the gutter; the end is nailed to the roof. Cover the nailheads with roofing compound.

replace the tape as soon as possible with pop rivets. Pop rivets, put in with a special pop-rivet tool, can be used directly on a hanging downspout or elbow. Hold the loose section in place and drill through both loose and attached sections at each side and at the front, using a drill with the size of bit that is specified by the pop-rivet manufacturer. To insert each rivet, place a rivet in the pop-rivet tool. Hold the drilled section of downspout in place, insert the tip of the rivet through the hole drilled on one side of the downspout sections, and squeeze the handles of the tool to set the rivet. Repeat for each fastening around the loose section.

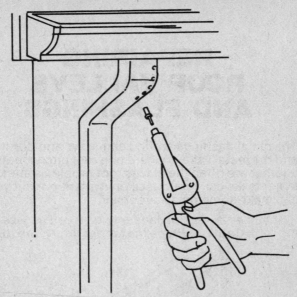

Pop rivets, installed with a special tool, can be used to reattach any loose sections of downspout or elbow. Hold the loose section in place and drill through both loose and attached sections at each side and at the front. Place a rivet in the special tool, hold the drilled section of downspout in place, insert the tip of the rivet, and squeeze the handles of the tool to set the rivet.

REPAIRING ROOF VALLEYS AND FLASHINGS

The metal flashings around chimneys and dormers and the metal valleys where one roof pitch meets another are often the places roof problems start. Major leaks call for professional attention, but you can make some repairs yourself.

Set up an extension ladder to give you access to the roof. **Caution:** *Brace the ladder firmly; the top of*

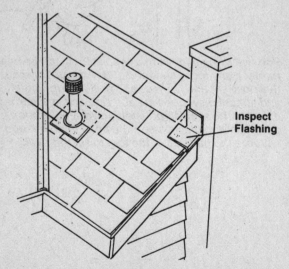

Inspect Flashing

It is a good idea to inspect all flashing and valley joints each spring. If the compound along a joint looks worn or thin, apply roofing compound generously. Inspect vent pipes and apply compound as necessary. If the protective collar at the base of a pipe is loose, knock it back against the pipe. Caulk around the collar.

the ladder should stick up above the edge of the roof. Wear old clothes and rubber-soled shoes.

Inspect flashing and valley joints each spring. If the roofing compound along a joint looks worn or you can see thin spots or gaps, apply roofing compound generously along the entire joint with a trowel. Make sure the compound covers both edges of the joined surfaces completely.

Chimney flashing is installed in two sections, the base and the cap. The cap flashing is embedded in the mortar joints between bricks. If the mortar holding it in place is beginning to crumble or the cap flashing has pulled loose from the masonry, remove the lip of the flashing completely from the mortar joint. Do not pull the flashing away from the chimney; leave it in place except for the loose edge.

Wearing safety goggles, remove the old mortar from the flashing joint; use a cold chisel and a sledgehammer to clean the joint completely. Be careful not to dislodge the chimney flashing any further. Wire-brush the chiseled-out joint to remove any remaining debris.

Mix cement mortar mix as directed. Dampen the cleaned joint with a wet paintbrush and fill the joint

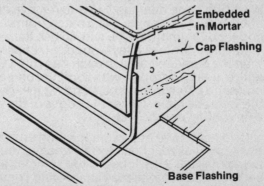

Embedded in Mortar

Cap Flashing

Base Flashing

Chimney flashing is installed in two sections, the base and the cap. The cap flashing is embedded in the mortar joints between bricks.

firmly with mortar, using a small sharp trowel; be careful not to leave any gaps. When the entire joint is filled, reset the lip of the flashing into the fresh mortar, pressing only hard enough to set it into place. If you press too hard, the flashing may spring back, pulling the new mortar out with it.

Let the newly mortared joint dry completely, according to the manufacturer's directions. Then caulk all around the top of the cap flashing with roof caulk where the lip of the flashing meets the mortar joint.

Inspect vent pipes and apply roofing compound as necessary. If the protective collar at the base of the pipe is loose, knock it back against the pipe with the shaft of a screwdriver. Caulk around the collar with roof caulk.

Valley flashings, used where two roof pitches meet, are either open or closed. An open flashing is left uncovered; the metal shows all along the valley. A closed flashing is covered with shingles. You'll be able to see damage to open valleys; you'll also be able to repair them. Damaged closed valleys are indicated by leaks inside, directly under the valleys; they usually require professional attention.

Small holes in open valleys are easy to patch. Wire-brush the damaged area to remove dirt and debris. Using tin snips, cut a patch from sheet copper or aluminum—be sure to use the same metal used for the valley—about 4 inches longer than the damaged area in each direction. Coat the entire area generously with roofing compound and press the patch into place, bending it to conform to the valley's shape. Cover the edges of the patch with roofing compound.

If you can't see any damage along an open valley but it has leaked, check to see whether the shingles along the valley are loose. If the shingles are loose, set them back into place with roofing compound, applied generously; work from the bottom up. If the shingles are still firmly secured, the flashing may be too narrow; call a professional.